MOST ASKED
QUESTIONS
about the
SOCIETY
OF SAINT PIUS X

MOST ASKED
QUESTIONS

about the

SOCIETY OF
SAINT PIUS X

Revised and Updated
2nd Edition

ANGELUS PRESS
2915 FOREST AVENUE
KANSAS CITY, MISSOURI 64109

ANGELUS PRESS
2915 FOREST AVENUE
KANSAS CITY, MISSOURI 64109
PHONE (816) 753-3150
FAX (816) 753-3557
ORDER LINE 1-800-966-7337
www.angeluspress.org

ISBN 978-1-892331-89-2 .
FIRST EDITION—1997
SECOND EDITION—March 2011

Printed in the United States of America.

CONTENTS

Introduction

"[In the Church there has been] a turning away from God and a turning to the world, to man. The world is not converting to the Church; the 'Church' has converted to the world."

Many Catholics realize more or less acutely that the Church is passing through a period of confusion, and they wonder whether there are simple guidelines for seeing them through it. This booklet tries to present principles, hopefully of solution but at least of sanity (even if not perhaps the complete answers), to be these simple guidelines. Our Lord God, moreover, does not ask us to solve what He has not given eminent theologians to solve. He asks that we save our souls, which we do, with His grace, by living as well as we can as Catholics, as true sons of the One, Holy, Catholic, and Apostolic Church.

The origins of this period of confusion lie in the whole "face-lift" of the Church since the Second Vatican Council. The Church has a "new look":

- New catechisms
- New liturgy—new churches, around a table, with communion in the hand from lay ministers aided by altar-girls, *etc.*
- New Bibles and Canon Law
- Involvement with non-Catholics
- New orientations—world "justice," "peace," *etc.*
- Laymen doing what priests did, *etc.*

And what happened to:

- The traditional Latin Mass?
- Benediction of the Blessed Sacrament?
- Regular individual confessions?
- Processions?
- The Way of the Cross, Fast and Abstinence, Prayers for the Holy Souls, *etc.*?
- Religious and priests in their habits, *etc.*?

What has *not* changed in Catholic life? The question is: Is this truly just a "face-lift," or is it really an "about-face?"

The latter, answers the Society of Saint Pius X. It is a turning away from God and a turning to the world, to man. The world is not converting to the Church; the "Church" has converted to the world. Are modern Catholics very different from non-Catholics these days? Clearly not.

To judge rightly these goings-on in the Church, let us look first at some general principles that all Catholics accept (Part I), and then we can evaluate better the Society of Saint Pius X's reaction to this crisis (Part II).

True to our aim at simplicity, answers will be brief and even in note form. For fuller answers, further reading and study will be necessary (Appendix II). May this little work give to those who have no time or means for a longer look some answers to the questions they are asking.

N.B.: The General Principles will be referred to throughout this booklet by their number given in Part I (so the second, for example, will be called Principle 2); in like manner, the Questions in Part II will be referred to as *QUESTION #*.

The abbreviation Dz. refers to Denzinger's *The Sources of Catholic Dogma*, translated by Roy J. Deferrari from the Thirtieth Edition of Henry Denzinger's *Enchiridion Symbolorum* (1955; reprint: Loreto Publications, n.d.).

PART I: PRINCIPLES

*Guiding Principles
in Today's Crisis*

1. The Catholic Church is divine.

Moreover, in order that we may perform satisfactorily the duty of embracing the true faith and of continuously persevering in it, God, through His only-begotten Son, has instituted the Church and provided it with clear signs of His institution, so that it can be recognized by all as the guardian and teacher of the revealed word (Vatican I, Dz. 1793).

2. The Catholic Church is the unique ark of salvation.

The Catholic Church firmly believes, professes, and proclaims that those not living within Her, not only pagans, but also Jews, heretics, and schismatics, cannot become participants in eternal life but will depart "into everlasting fire which was prepared for the devil and his angels" (Mt. 25:41), unless before the end of life the same have been added to the flock... (Council of Florence, Dz. 714).

3. The Catholic Church is visible and indefectible.

Moreover, what the Chief of pastors and the Great Pastor of sheep, the Lord Jesus, established in the blessed Apostle Peter for the perpetual salvation and perennial good of the Church, this by the same Author must endure always in the Church which was founded upon a rock and will endure firm until the end of the ages. (Vatican I, Dz. 1824 [cf. Dz. 1793 above])

The one Church of Christ is visible to all and will remain, according to the Will of its Author, exactly the same as He instituted it. (Pius XI, *Mortalium Animos,* §15)

4. The Church is founded upon Peter and his successors forever.

If anyone then says that it is not from the institution of Christ the Lord Himself or by divine right that the blessed Peter has perpetual successors in the primacy over the universal Church...let him be anathema....

If anyone thus speaks, that the Roman Pontiff has only the office of inspection or direction but not the full and supreme power of jurisdiction over the universal Church, not only in things which pertain to faith and morals, but also in those which pertain to the discipline and government of the Church spread over the whole world...let him be anathema. (Vatican I, Dz. 1825, 1831)

But it is opposed to the truth and in evident contradiction with the divine constitution of the Church to hold that, while each bishop is individually bound to obey the authority of the Roman Pontiffs, taken collectively the bishops are not so bound. (Leo XIII, *Satis Cognitum*)

5. The Pope has power only "unto edification and not unto destruction" (II Cor. 13:10) of Christ's Church.

For, the Holy Spirit was not promised to the successors of Peter that by His revelation they might disclose new doctrine, but that by His help they might guard sacredly the revelation transmitted through the apostles and the deposit of faith, and might faithfully set it forth. (Vatican I, Dz. 1836)

And for these sacraments instituted by Christ the Lord, in the course of the ages the Church has not and could not substitute other sacraments, since, as the Council of Trent teaches, the seven sacraments of the New Law have all been instituted by Jesus Christ our Lord and the Church has no power over the "substance of the sacraments," that is, over those things which, with the sources of divine revelation as witnesses, Christ the Lord Himself decreed to be preserved in a sacramental sign.... (Pius XII, *Sacramentum Ordinis,* Dz. 2301)

It is well known unto all men...with what great care and pastoral vigilance our predecessors the Roman Pontiffs have discharged the office entrusted by Christ Our Lord to them in the person of the most blessed Peter, Prince of the Apostles, have unremittingly discharged the duty of feeding the lambs and the sheep, and have diligently nourished the Lord's entire flock with the words of faith, imbued it with salutary doctrine, and guarded it from poisoned pastures. And those our predecessors, who were the assertors and champions of the august Catholic religion, of truth and justice, being as they were chiefly solicitous for the salvation of souls, held nothing to be of so great importance as the duty of exposing and condemning, in their most wise Letters and Constitutions, all heresies and errors which are hostile to moral honesty and to the eternal salvation of mankind.... (Pius IX, *Quanta Cura,* §1)

6. Church teaching cannot change.

Revelation, constituting the object of Catholic faith, was not completed with the apostles. (Condemned by St. Pius X, *Lamentabili,* Dz. 2021)

Further, by divine and Catholic faith, all those things must be believed which are contained in the written word of God and in Tradition, and which are proposed by the Church, either in a solemn pronouncement or in her ordinary and universal teaching power, to be believed as divinely revealed....

...Hence, also, that understanding of its sacred dogmas must be perpetually retained, which Holy Mother Church has once declared; and there must never be recession from that meaning under the specious name of a deeper understanding.

...[D]efinitions of the Roman Pontiff from himself, but not from the consensus of the Church, are unalterable. (Vatican I, Dz. 1792, 1800, 1839)

7. Protestants and other non-Catholics don't have the Faith.

Now it is manifest that he who adheres to the teaching of the Church, as to an infallible rule, assents to whatever the Church teaches; otherwise, if, of the things taught by the Church, he holds what he chooses to hold, and rejects what he chooses to reject, he no longer adheres to the teaching of the Church as to an infallible rule, but to his own will....Therefore it is clear that such a heretic with regard to one article has no faith in the other articles, but only a kind of opinion in accordance with his own will. (St. Thomas Aquinas, *Summa Theologica,* II-II, Q. 5, Art. 3)

8. Human law is ordained to divine law.

Likewise the liberty of those who are in authority does not consist in the power to lay unreasonable and capricious commands upon their subjects...but the binding force of human laws is in this, that they are to be regarded as applications of the eternal law, and incapable of sanctioning anything which is not contained in the eternal law, as in the principle of all law. (Leo XIII, *Libertas,* §10)

9. Bad laws are no laws.

If, then, by any one in authority, something be sanctioned out of conformity with the principles of right reason, and consequently hurtful to the commonwealth, such an enactment can have no binding force of law, as being no rule of justice, but certain to lead men away from that good which is the very end of civil society....But where the power to command is wanting, or where a law is enacted contrary to reason, or to the eternal law, or to some ordinance of God, obedience is unlawful, lest, while obeying man, we become disobedient to God. (Leo XIII, *Libertas* §§10, 13)

10. In certain circumstances ecclesiastical laws do not oblige.

a) WHEN DOUBTFUL: "When there is a doubt of law, laws do not bind even if they be nullifying and disqualifying ones..." (1917 Code of Canon Law, canon 15; 1983 Code of Canon Law, canon 14).

b) WHEN RETROACTIVE: "A law comes into existence when it is promulgated" (1917 Code of Canon Law, canon 8, §1 [cf. canon 17, §2]; 1983 Code of Canon Law, canon 7 [cf. canon 16, §2]).

c) WHEN THEY CANNOT BE OBSERVED (physically or morally): "No positive law obliges where there is grave inconvenience" is a principle of moral theology (cf. 1917 Code of Canon Law, canon 2205, §2; 1983 Code of Canon Law, canon 1323, §4). There certainly is such a grave inconvenience when observance would be detrimental to souls, for "the salvation of souls must always be the supreme law of the Church" (1983 Code of Canon Law, canon 1752).

11. The Mass is not essentially a meal.

If anyone says that in the Mass a true and real sacrifice is not offered to God, or that the act of offering is nothing else than Christ being given to us to eat, let him be anathema. (Council of Trent, Dz. 948)

12. The Mass is the re-enactment of Calvary (and not just a narrative of the Last Supper, which was itself but a pre-enactment of Calvary).

He, therefore, our God and Lord, though He was about to offer Himself once to God the Father upon the altar of the Cross...nevertheless, that His sacerdotal office might not come to an end with His death, at the Last Supper, on the night He was betrayed, so that He might leave to His beloved spouse the Church a visible sacrifice (as the nature of man demands), whereby that bloody sacrifice once to be completed on the Cross might be represented, and the memory of it remain even to the end of the world...offered to God the Father His own body and blood under the species of bread and wine.... (Council of Trent, Dz. 950)

13. The Mass is not a community gathering.

If anyone says that Masses in which the priest alone communicates sacramentally, are illicit and are therefore to be abrogated, let him be anathema. (Council of Trent, Dz. 955; cf. Principle 14)

14. The prayers of the Mass are not directed to the people but to God.

If anyone says that the rite of the Roman Church, according to which a part of the canon and the words of consecration are pronounced in a low tone, is to be condemned..., let him be anathema. (Council of Trent, Dz. 956)

15. Holy Communion under both species is not necessary for the laity.

If anyone denies that the whole Christ is contained in the venerable sacrament of the Eucharist under each species and under every part of each species, when the separation has been made, let him be anathema. (Council of Trent, Dz. 885)

If anyone says that the holy Catholic Church has not been influenced by just causes and reasons to give communion under the form of bread only to laymen and even to clerics when not consecrating, or that she has erred in this, let him be anathema. (Council of Trent, Dz. 935)

16. The Blessed Sacrament is Our Lord and must be worshipped.

If anyone says that in the holy sacrament of the Eucharist the only-begotten Son of God is not to be adored even outwardly with the worship of *latria*...let him be anathema. (Council of Trent, Dz. 888)

17. The Blessed Sacrament contains the whole Christ under the species of bread and wine.

If anyone denies that in the sacrament of the most holy Eucharist there are truly, really, and substantially contained the body and blood together with the soul and divinity of our Lord Jesus Christ, and therefore the whole Christ, but shall say that He is in it as by a sign or figure, or force, let him be anathema. (Council of Trent, Dz. 883)

18. The Catholic priesthood is of divine origin.

If anyone says that by these words: "Do this for a commemoration of me," (Lk. 22:19; I Cor. 11:24), Christ did not make the Apostles priests, or did not ordain that they and other priests might offer His own body and blood: let him be anathema. (Council of Trent, Dz. 949)

19. The traditional Latin Mass is still in force in virtue of *Quo Primum*:

By these present (ordinances) and by virtue of Our Apostolic Authority, We give and grant in perpetuity that for the singing or reading of Mass in any church whatsoever this Missal may be followed absolutely, without any scruple of conscience or fear of incurring any penalty, judgment or censure, and may be freely and lawfully used....We likewise order and declare that no one whosoever shall be forced or coerced into altering this Missal; and that this present Constitution can never be revoked or modified, but shall forever remain valid and have the force of law.... (St. Pius V, *Quo Primum*)

AS IMMEMORIAL CUSTOM:[1] "...unless it makes express mention of centenary or immemorial customs, a law does not revoke them..." (1917 Code of Canon Law, canon 30; 1983 Code of Canon Law, canon 28); **and because the *Novus Ordo Missae* is not to be regarded as an option open to faithful Catholics:**

1. The accompanying *Critical Study* is the work of a select group of bishops, theologians, liturgists and pastors of souls. Despite its brevity, the study shows quite clearly that the *Novus Ordo Missae*—considering the new elements susceptible to widely different interpretations which are implied or taken for granted—represents, both as a whole and in its details, a striking departure from the Catholic theology of the Mass as it was formulated in Session 22 of the Council of Trent. The "canons" of the rite definitively fixed at that time erected an insurmountable barrier against any heresy which might attack the integrity of the Mystery....

---

[1] The traditional Latin Mass is a custom at least 1,500 years old.

To abandon a liturgical tradition which for four centuries stood as a sign and pledge of unity in worship, and to replace it with another liturgy which, due to the countless liberties it implicitly authorizes, cannot but be a sign of division—a liturgy which teems with insinuations or manifest errors against the integrity of the Catholic Faith—is, we feel bound in conscience to proclaim, an incalculable error. (Cardinals Ottaviani and Bacci, *Short Critical Study of the New Order of Mass,* pp. 27, 55)

The Apostolic Letter *Summorum Pontificum,* on the use of the Roman Liturgy prior to the reform of 1970, issued on July 7, 2007, also addresses this question:

It is, therefore, permissible to celebrate the Sacrifice of the Mass following the typical edition of the Roman Missal promulgated by Bl. John XXIII in 1962 and never abrogated, as an extraordinary form of the Liturgy of the Church. (Art. 1)

PART II: QUESTIONS

*Leading Questions about the
Society of St. Pius X*

I

Who was Archbishop Marcel Lefebvre?

November 29, 1905

> Birth of Marcel Lefebvre into a good Catholic family (five of the eight children would become priests or nuns).

September 21, 1929

> Marcel Lefebvre is ordained a priest.

1932 - 1946

> Having become a Holy Ghost Father, he becomes a missionary in Gabon, Africa.

September 18, 1947

He is consecrated a bishop and appointed Apostolic Vicar of Dakar, Senegal.

1948 - 1959

Bishop Lefebvre is Pope Pius XII's Apostolic Delegate for eighteen African countries.

September 14, 1955

He becomes the first Archbishop of Dakar.

1962 - 1969

His Grace returns to France to be the Bishop of Tulle.

1968

Archbishop Lefebvre is elected and acts as Superior General of the Holy Ghost Fathers until resigning before the changes his Congregation would force him to implement, and going into "retirement."

1969

The Archbishop founds the Priestly Society of Saint Pius X.

1970 - 1982

He acts as its first Superior General.

1970 -1988

Archbishop Lefebvre does all he can to be faithful to the grace of his episcopacy, traveling the world to encourage Catholics to hold fast to the Faith and traditions of their fathers, confirming their young and ordaining for them priests.

June 30, 1988

> In view of his imminent death, he consecrates successors.

March 25, 1991

> Archbishop Marcel Lefebvre passes before his Eternal Judge.

A Testimony

Concerning the Archbishop personally, a journalist asked recently what was my outstanding memory of the man. I gave maybe a surprising answer: his objectivity. He had, of course, a uniquely attractive personality because he was a saint—gentle, kind, simple, humble, humorous, and so on, without a trace of sentimentality, but that was not the point. Underneath all that lay a great intelligence and faith and firmness of character, but that was still not the point. Essentially he was a man empty of self and full of God. To meet him, to talk to him, was to see—through him—the truth, Our Lord Jesus Christ, the Catholic Church. He was like a window on the interest of God. Not he, but Christ, lived within him, and yet that was Marcel Lefebvre and nobody else. And what a marvelous man he was![1]

---

[1]   Bishop Richard Williamson, *The Angelus*, May-June 1991, p. 2.

II

What is the Society of St. Pius X?

1969

A "retired" archbishop, Msgr. Marcel Lefebvre, agrees to help a handful of young seminarians who are disconcerted by the direction being taken in post-Vatican II seminaries in their priestly formation. He does this, not only by undertaking their training, but also by founding a Society aiming at fostering a priestly life according to the wise norms and customs of the Church of previous days.

November 1, 1970

The Society of Saint Pius X is officially recognized by the Bishop of Lausanne, Geneva, and Fribourg,

Bishop Charrière. It is therefore truly a new little branch pushed forth by the Church.

February 18, 1971

Cardinal Wright, Prefect of the Sacred Congregation for the Clergy, issues a decree praising the wisdom of the Society's statutes.

June 10, 1971

Archbishop Lefebvre announces, together with the staff of the Seminary of Saint Pius X at Ecône, the refusal to adopt the *Novus Ordo Missae* (cf. *QUESTION 5*).

1971 - 1974

Following on Cardinal Wright's letter are other sure signs of Rome's full acceptance of the Society of Saint Pius X:

1. Allowing its houses to be erected canonically in one Italian and two Swiss dioceses.
2. Allowing three outside priests to join the Society and to be incardinated[1] directly into it. During the same years the French Episcopal Conference was maneuvering to have the Society and its seminary suppressed (cf. *QUESTION 3*).

November 1, 1980

By its tenth anniversary, the Society of Saint Pius X has forty houses on two continents.

---

[1] **incardinated**. Accepted by the Church as being a cleric belonging either to a diocese or to a religious institute. Without incardination a cleric is a "vagabond" and has no right to exercise his ministry.

November 1, 2010

By its fortieth anniversary, the Society of Saint Pius X numbers 4 bishops, 529 priests, 233 seminarians, 104 brothers, about 160 sisters, and 73 oblates, living in 183 houses in 32 countries. Together they seek the goal of the priesthood: the glorification of God, the continuation of Our Lord's redemptive work, the salvation of souls. They accomplish this by fidelity to Christ's testament—the Holy Sacrifice of the Mass (see Appendix III).

III

Wasn't the Society of St. Pius X lawfully suppressed?

November 1, 1970

The Society is lawfully and canonically founded (*QUESTION 2*).

1971-1974

Nevertheless, the French bishops, balking at Ecône's pre-Vatican II ways, and notably at its non-acceptance of the *Novus Ordo Missae* (*QUESTION 5*), calumniate it as *sauvage* (*outlaw, rebel*). One of them, Pope Paul VI's Secretary of State, Cardinal Villot, deceives the

Holy Father into believing Archbishop Lefebvre had his priests sign a declaration against the Pope.[1]

November 11-13, 1974

An Apostolic Visitation of the seminary at Ecône takes place. This is in itself normal procedure; its conclusions, though never published, were "very favorable," according to Cardinal Garonne, "except that you don't use the new liturgy, and there's a somewhat anti-conciliar spirit there."[2] The Visitors, however, scandalized everyone by their unorthodox views, prompting Archbishop Lefebvre's so-called *Declaration* (see Appendix I).

February 13 and March 3, 1975

Archbishop Lefebvre meets with an improvised Commission of three Cardinals, nominally to discuss the Apostolic Visitation but in fact as a lone defendant before a tribunal attacking his Declaration. Having been given no warning as to the nature of these "trials," he has no lawyer and is never allowed a copy of the recorded meetings, though that at least is promised him.

May 6, 1975

The irregular Commission of Cardinals condemns Archbishop Lefebvre, finding his Declaration "unacceptable on all points." They write to Bishop Mamie (successor of Bishop Charrière at Fribourg) telling him to withdraw his predecessor's approval of the Society of Saint Pius X—something quite beyond his power. (Once a bishop has approved a Society, only

---

[1] Archbishop Lefebvre, *Fideliter,* No. 59, pp. 68-70.
[2] *Ibid.,* p. 67.

the Pope can suppress it. Cf. 1917 Code of Canon Law, canon 493.)

June 5, 1975

Archbishop Lefebvre *submits an appeal* to the Apostolic Signatura in Rome—in substance:

> it would be for the Sacred Congregation for the Doctrine of the Faith to determine whether my Declaration were at fault. Please provide evidence that this Commission of Cardinals had been expressly mandated by the Pope (who by his own authority can bypass the Congregations) to decide as has been done.[3] And if I be at fault, of course I can be censured, but not the Society which was founded in due canonical form.

Cardinal Villot arranges that the appeal is not accepted. Cardinal Staffa is threatened with dismissal if he dare to accept an appeal from Archbishop Lefebvre.[4]

June 29, 1975

Pope Paul VI is persuaded to write to Archbishop Lefebvre that he approved of all the actions of the Commission of Cardinals. (It is impossible that mere papal approbation in June could empower this Commission which had met the previous February [Principle 10b].)

On this whole process, Archbishop Lefebvre observes:

> We have been condemned without trial, without opportunity to defend ourselves, without due warning or written process and without appeal."[5]

---

[3] This evidence was never produced. A doubt about the validity of a law excuses from observing it (Principle 10a). How much the more does doubt about the authority of the legislator!

[4] *Vatican Encounter*, pp. 185 and 191 (Appendix II).

[5] *Open Letter to Confused Catholics*, p. 150 (Appendix II).

Over and above the canonical question, there remains that of natural law. Must one observe a censure when no crime can be pointed out or when the very authority not to mention the identity of the judge is unsure?

IV

Wasn't Archbishop Lefebvre suspended from performing all sacred functions along with the priests ordained?

Nov. 1, 1970

The Society is lawfully and canonically founded (*QUESTION 2*).

Oct. 27, 1975

Cardinal Villot writes to the hierarchies of the world to tell them no longer to incardinate[1] any priests from the Society of Saint Pius X, as it has been suppressed.[2]

---

[1] Cf. *Question 2*, n. 1.
[2] Cf. Michael Davies, *Apologia Pro Marcel Lefebvre*, I, 136.

June 12, 1976

Msgr. Benelli writes Archbishop Lefebvre, telling him not to ordain priests without their local bishops' permission.

June 29, 1976

Archbishop Lefebvre goes ahead with the foreseen ordinations.

July 1, 1976

The "suspension" of Archbishop Lefebvre and his newly ordained priests is declared.

A First Observation

The Church, by approving the Society of Saint Pius X, approved also that it live, *i.e.*, that it have all the ordinary means to lead its religious life and fulfill its aim. This is a fundamental consideration when taking into consideration the nullity of its suppression (*QUESTION 3*).

Moreover:

- Then again, the Society of Saint Pius X not being lawfully suppressed, it was unjust to try to stop candidates from joining it.

- After Cardinal Wright's letter of praise, the Congregation for the Clergy's allowing religious priests transferring to the Society to be directly incardinated into it, and Bishop Adam's (of Sion) judging that the Society, being inter-diocesan, could generalize this procedure, Archbishop Lefebvre could reasonably presume this right of incardination.[3] So the real problem was more than canonical.

---

[3] *The Angelus*, April 1987, p. 3 (*Fideliter*, No. 55, p. 3 ff.).

Primarily, it is an attack on the traditional Latin Mass

In the three weeks before the ordinations to be held on June 29, 1976, Archbishop Lefebvre was approached by Rome as many as six times with the request that he establish normal relations with the Vatican and that he give proof of this by saying a Mass according to the new rite. He was told that if the ordination Mass on the 29th would be with the Missal of Pope Paul VI, then all opposition would be smoothed over. This offer was brought to the Archbishop on the vigil of the Feast. One *Novus Ordo Missae* and all would be well. Herein we see most clearly the *one fundamental reason for the campaign against Archbishop Lefebvre and his Society: exclusive adhesion to the old Mass and refusal to say the new.*

But:

- the *Novus Ordo Missae* cannot be said (cf. *QUESTION 5*)
- and the old Mass always can (Principle 20).

Therefore, the *suspensions are null:*

- canonically, because unjust,
- fundamentally, because engineered to do away with the traditional Latin Mass.

But even if *unjust*, shouldn't censures be *observed?*

- If only the one incurring them were to suffer, then YES, that is the more perfect way to act.
- If there is a question of depriving innumerable souls of the graces they need for salvation, then NO, one cannot.

Before such an unjust campaign of suppression, the Society could only continue.

Rome, moreover, has always tacitly recognized the Society of Saint Pius X's legitimate continuation (for example, in May 1988, when Cardinal Ratzinger agreed to the principle of having a bishop consecrated from among the Society's priests) and the nullity of the suspensions (for example, when, in December 1987, Cardinal Gagnon did not hesitate to attend as a prelate the Mass of the "suspended" Archbishop).

V

Why should Catholics have nothing to do with the Novus Ordo Missae?

A) Preliminary Remarks

A criticism of the "New Rite" cannot be a criticism of the Mass in itself, for this is the very sacrifice of Our Lord bequeathed to His Church, but it is an examination, whether it is a fit rite for embodying and enacting this august Sacrifice.

It is difficult for those who have known nothing other than the *Novus Ordo Missae* to understand what they have been deprived of—and attending a "Latin Mass" often just seems alien. To see clearly what it is all about, it is necessary to have a clear understanding of the defined truths of our Faith on the Mass (Principles 11-18 are some of them). Only in the light of these can the "new rite" of Mass be evaluated.

B) What is the *Novus Ordo Missae*?

Let us answer this by looking at its four causes, as the philosophers would say:

(i) What are the ELEMENTS that make up the New Rite?
Some are Catholic—a priest, bread and wine, genuflections, signs of the cross, *etc.*, but some are Protestant—a table, commonplace utensils, communion in the hand, *etc.*

(ii) Now, the *Novus Ordo Missae* assumes these heterodox elements alongside the Catholic ones to form a LITURGY FOR A MODERNIST RELIGION which would marry the Church and the world, Catholicism and Protestantism, light and darkness. Indeed, the *Novus Ordo Missae* presents itself as:

- **a meal** (vs. Principle 11). This is shown by its use of a table around which the people of God gather to offer bread and wine (vs. Principle 18) and to communicate from rather common-place utensils, often under both kinds (vs. Principle 15), and usually in the hand (vs. Principle 16). (Note too the almost complete deletion of references to sacrifice).

- **a narrative of a past event** (vs. Principle 12). This told out loud by the one presiding (vs. Principle 14), who recounts Our Lord's words as read in Scripture (rather than pronouncing a sacramental formula) and who makes no pause until he has shown the Host to the people.

- **a community gathering**, (vs. Principle 13). Christ is perhaps considered to be morally present but ignored in his Sacramental Presence (vs. Principles 16 and 17).

(iii) Notice also the numerous RUBRICAL CHANGES: the celebrant facing the people from where the tabernacle was formerly kept.

- Just after the consecration, all acclaim He "will come again."

- Sacred vessels are no longer gilt.

- Sacred particles are ignored (vs. Principle 15):

  - The priest no longer joins thumb and forefinger after the consecration.

  - The vessels are not purified as they used to be.

  - Communion is most frequently given in the hand.

- Genuflections on the part of the priest and kneeling on the part of the faithful are much reduced.

- The people take over much of what the priest formerly did.

Moreover, the *Novus Ordo Missae* defined itself this way:

> The Lord's Supper, or Mass, is a sacred synaxis, or assembly of the people of God gathered together under the presidency of the priest to celebrate the memorial of the Lord.[1]

(iv) What is the AIM of this *Novus Ordo Missae* as a rite?

> ...the *intention of Pope Paul VI* with regard to what is commonly called the Mass, was to reform the Catholic liturgy in such a way that it should almost *coincide with the Protestant liturgy*...there was with Pope Paul VI an ecumenical intention to remove, or at least to correct, or at least to relax, what was too Catholic, in the traditional sense, in the Mass and, I repeat, to get the Catholic Mass closer to the Calvinist mass....[2]

> When I began work on this trilogy I was concerned at the extent to which the Catholic liturgy was being Protestantized. The more detailed my study of the Revolution, the more evident it has become that it has by-passed Protestantism and its *final goal is humanism.*[3]

---

[1] Pope Paul VI, *Institutio Generalis,* §7, 1969 version.

[2] Jean Guitton (Dec. 19, 1993) *Apropos* (17) p. 8 f. [*Christian Order,* Oct. 1994] Jean Guitton was an intimate friend of Pope Paul VI. Paul VI had 116 of his books and had made marginal study notes in 17 of these.

[3] *Pope Paul's New Mass,* p. 137 (cf. p. 149), (see Appendix II).

This latter is a fair evaluation when one considers the changes implemented, the results achieved, and the tendency of modern theology, even papal theology (cf. Question 7).

(v) Who made up the *Novus Ordo Missae?*

It is the invention of a liturgical commission, the Consilium, whose guiding light was Fr. Annibale Bugnini (made an archbishop in 1972 for his services), and which also included six Protestant experts. Father Bugnini (principal author of Vatican II's *Sacrosanctum Concilium*) had his own ideas on popular involvement in the liturgy,[4] and the Protestant advisors had their own heretical ideas on the essence of the Mass.

But the one on whose authority the *Novus Ordo Missae* was enforced was Pope Paul VI, who "promulgated" it by his constitution *Missale Romanum* (April 3, 1969).

(vi) Or did POPE PAUL VI really do so?

- In the original version of *Missale Romanum*, signed by Pope Paul VI, no mention was made either of anyone's being obliged to use the *Novus Ordo Missae* or when such an obligation might begin.

- Translators of the constitution mistranslate *cogere et efficere* (*i.e., to sum up and draw a conclusion*) as *to give force of law.*

- The version in the *Acta Apostolicae Sedis* has an added paragraph "enjoining" the New Missal, but it is in the wrong tense, the past, and reads *praescripsimus* (*i.e., which we have ordered*) thereby referring to a past obligation, and nothing, moreover, in *Missale Romanum* prescribes, but at most permits the use of the "New Rite."[5]

---

[4] A. Bugnini, *La Riforma Liturgica* (Centro Liturgico Vincenziano, 1983).
[5] *The Angelus*, March 1997, p. 35.

Can it be true that Pope Paul VI wanted this Missal but that it was not properly imposed?[6]

C) Judgment on the *Novus Ordo Missae*

(i) Judging the *Novus Ordo Missae* in itself, in its official Latin form, Cardinals Ottaviani and Bacci wrote to Pope Paul VI that "the *Novus Ordo* represents, both as a whole and in its details, a striking departure from the Catholic theology of the Mass as it was formulated in Session XXIII of the Council of Trent" (September 25, 1969). And Archbishop Lefebvre definitely agreed with them when he wrote:

> The *Novus Ordo Missae*, even when said with piety and respect for the liturgical rules, ...is impregnated with the spirit of Protestantism. It bears within it a poison harmful to the faith.[7]

The dissimulation of Catholic elements and the pandering to Protestants which are evident in the *Novus Ordo Missae* render it a danger to our faith, and, as such, evil, given that it lacks the good which the sacred rite of Mass ought to have.

(ii) By their fruits you shall know them:

We were promised the *Novus Ordo Missae* would renew Catholic fervor, inspire the young, draw back the lapsed and attract non-Catholics. Who today can pretend that these things are its fruits? Together with the *Novus Ordo Missae* did there not instead come a dramatic decline in Mass attendance and vocations, an "identity crisis" among priests, a slowing in the rate of conversions, and an acceleration of apostasies?

So, from the point of view of its fruits, the *Novus Ordo Missae* is not a rite conducive to the flourishing of the Church's mission.

---

[6] It is known, moreover, that Pope Paul VI signed the *Institutio Generalis* without reading it and without ensuring that it had been checked out by the Holy Office.

[7] *An Open Letter to Confused Catholics*, p. 29 (Appendix II).

(iii) Does it follow from the apparent promulgation by the Popes that the *Novus Ordo Missae* is truly Catholic? No, for the indefectibility of the Church does not prevent the Pope personally from promoting defective and modernist rites in the Latin rite of the Church. Moreover, the *Novus Ordo Missae*:

- is not forced upon the Church, as the Traditional Latin Mass can always be said (Principle 19),

- is not promulgated regularly (cf. [vi] above),

- and does not engage the Church's infallibility.[8]

D) This being so, can it be said that the *Novus Ordo Missae* is invalid?

This does not necessarily follow from the above defects, as serious as they might be, for only three things are required for validity: matter, form, and intention.

However, the celebrant must intend to do what the Church does. The *Novus Ordo Missae* will no longer in and of itself guarantee that the celebrant has this intention. That will depend on his personal faith (generally unknown to those assisting, but more and more doubtful as the crisis in the Church is prolonged). Therefore, these Masses can be of doubtful validity, and more so with time.

The words of consecration, especially of the wine, have been tampered with. Has the "substance of the sacrament" (cf. Pope Pius XII quoted in Principle 5) been respected? This is even more of a

---

[8] Let us remember that a Pope engages his infallibility not only when teaching on faith or morals (or legislating on what is necessarily connected with them) but when so doing with full pontifical authority and definitively (cf. Vatican I [Dz. 1839]). But as regards the *Novus Ordo Missae*, Pope Paul VI has stated (Nov. 19, 1969) that:

"the rite and its related rubric are not in themselves a dogmatic definition. They are capable of various theological qualifications, depending on the liturgical context to which they relate. They are gestures and terms relating to a lived and living religious action which involves the ineffable mystery of God's presence; it is an action that is not always carried out in the exact same form, an action that only theological analysis can examine and express in doctrinal formulas that are logically satisfying."

problem in Masses in the vernacular, where *pro multis* (for many) is deliberately mistranslated as *for all*. Some argue that this is of such importance as to render these Masses invalid. Many deny it; but this change does add to the doubt.

E) Attendance

If the *Novus Ordo Missae* is not truly Catholic, then it *cannot oblige* for one's Sunday obligation. Many Catholics who do assist at it are unaware of its all pervasive degree of serious innovation and are exempt from guilt. However, any Catholic who is aware of its harm, does not have the right to participate. He could only then assist at it by a mere physical presence without positively taking part in it, and then for major family reasons (weddings, funerals, *etc.*).

VI

What are Catholics to think of the Second Vatican Council?

The Second Vatican Council was a meeting of the world's bishops for four sessions between October 11, 1962, and December 8, 1965. Pope John XXIII, in his opening speech to the Council (Nov. 11, 1962), declared its aims to be the following:

- that the Catholic faith should be kept and taught,

- but taught in the language of modern man by a magisterium "which is predominantly pastoral in character,"

- and this without resorting to any condemnations,

- thus appealing to all peoples. (This Council was to be ecumenical, not only in the sense of being a general council of the Church, but also in that of appealing to the religiosity of all people of whatever religion.)

Pope Paul VI agreed with his predecessor:

[Vatican II] was the most important [event] because...above all it sought to meet pastoral needs and, nourishing the flame of charity, it has made a great effort to reach not only the Christians still separated from communion with the Holy See, but also the whole human family. (Closing Brief, December 8, 1965).

With such ideals, it is little wonder to find Catholic teaching presented:

- weakly (no definitions or condemnations),
- confusedly (no technical, scholastic terminology),
- and one-sidedly (so as to attract non-Catholics).

All such vague and ambiguous teaching, already liberal in its method, would be interpreted in its true liberal sense after the Council. Consider the examples in the table on p. 47:

More gravely, the Council was hijacked by the liberal elements within the Church, who from the very beginning schemed to have rejected the pre-Conciliar preparatory schemas and replaced by progressive ones prepared by their own "experts." The liberals were also able to get their members onto the Council Commissions. The new schemas, passed as the Council's decrees, constitutions, and declarations, contain, more or less explicitly, some of the same doctrinal errors for which liberals in the past had been condemned. Let us take by way of example the following passages in the table on pp. 48-49.

The Council itself both encouraged liberal trends (and its encouragement became post-conciliar Vatican policy) and departed from traditional Catholic teaching, but it has no authority for either (Principle 5).

Conciliar Teaching	How Interpreted by Rome[1]
The liturgy of the word is stressed (*Sacrosanctum Concilium*,[2] §9), and the banquet aspect (§10), as well as active participation (§§11, 14), and therefore the vernacular (§§36, 54).	The *Novus Ordo Missae* (cf. *QUESTION 5*)
Catholics should pray with Protestants (*Unitatis Redintegratio*, §§4, 8).	Eucharistic Hospitality (cf. *QUESTION 8*).
The Church of Christ subsists in (*i.e.*, is not the same as) the Catholic Church (*Lumen Gentium*, §8),	It is also in "separated Churches" (*Ut Unum Sint*,[3] §11).
which has separated brethren in separated "Churches" (*Unitatis Redintegratio*, §3),	All the baptized are in Christ's Church (*Ut Unum Sint*, §42),
which ought to be as sisters (*Unitatis Redintegratio*, §14).	and so there is no need to convert non-Catholics, *e.g.*, the Orthodox.[4]
Seminarians should take into account modern philosophy, progress in science (*Optatam Totius*, §15),	Secular University studies and abandoning Thomism,
psychology, and sociology (§20).	open spirituality and subjective morality.
Marriage and married love equated (*Gaudium et Spes*, §§48, 50).	Annulments fiasco (cf. *QUESTION 8*).
The Church renounces privileges civil authorities grant her (§76).	Catholic religion no longer to be the religion of any State.
Wish for a world authority (§82).	Full support for United Nations.
Rite and formulae of penance are to be revised (*Sacrosanctum Concilium* §72).	Face to face confessions and general absolutions.[5]
Extreme Unction should be an anointing of the sick (§§73, 75).	New matter, form, and subject (*i.e.*, the sick, not just the dying).

[1] How Rome's guidelines are further interpreted as seen in the parishes is a whole other story.

[2] The documents of Vatican II are referred to by their introductory Latin words, or by the initials of these.

[3] *Ut Unum Sint,* Pope John Paul II, May 25, 1995.

[4] Cf. the Joint International Commission for the Theological Dialogue between the Roman Catholic Church and the Orthodox Church—which forbade mutual "prosleytizing." Balamand, Lebanon, 17 to 24 June 1993.

[5] Does this affect the "substance of the sacraments" over which the Church has no power? (Cf. Pius XII, quoted in Principle 5 above.)

Vatican II Teaching

"Man is the only creature on earth that God has wanted for its own sake" (*Gaudium et Spes*, §24),

and "all things on earth should be ordained to man" (§12).

Moreover, "by His incarnation the Son of God has in a certain way united himself with each man" (§22),

so "Human nature...has been raised in us also to a dignity beyond compare" (§22),

and because of "the sublime dignity of the human person" (§26),

his "rights and duties are universal and inviolate" (§26); including:

"The Vatican Council declares that the human person has a right to religious freedom..." (*Dignitatis Humanae,* §2),

"...all men should be immune from coercion on the part of...every human power so that, within due limits, nobody is forced to act against his convictions nor is anyone to be restrained from acting in accordance with his convictions..." (§2),

"This right of the human person to religious freedom must be given such recognition in the constitutional order of society as will make it a civil right" (§2),

"...the Spirit of Christ has not refrained from using (separated churches) as means of salvation" (*Unitatis Redintegratio,* §3), and so,

"ecumenical action should be encouraged so that...Catholics might cooperate with their separated brethren...by a common profession before the nations of faith in God and in Jesus Christ..." (*Ad Gentes,* §115).

Why, even concerning non-Christian religions: "The Catholic Church rejects nothing of what is good and holy in these religions. She has a high regard for the manner of life and conduct..." (*Nostra Aetate,* §2),

"Together with their head, the Supreme Pontiff, and never apart from him, they (the Bishops) have supreme and full authority over the universal Church..." (*Lumen Gentium,* §22).

"Now, episcopal consecration confers, together with the office of sanctifying, the duty also of teaching and ruling..." (§21).

CATHOLIC TEACHING

"The Lord hath made all things for Himself" (Prov. 16),

...to help him to save his soul.

God assumed an individual nature (*e.g.*, Dz. 114),

...a little less than the angels...(Ps. 8:6).

Only he who lives well is worthy (Apoc. 3:4).

He who buries his talent will be stripped of it.

Contrary condemned statement: "Liberty of conscience and of worship is the proper right of every man..." (Pius IX, *Quanta Cura*).

Contrary condemned statement: ...the best condition of society is the one in which there is no acknowledgment by the government of the duty of restraining...offenders of the Catholic religion, except insofar as the public peace demands" (Pius IX, *Quanta Cura*).

Contrary condemned statement: "Liberty of conscience and of worship... should be proclaimed and asserted by law in every correctly established society..." (Pius IX, *Quanta Cura*).

Principle 2

Principle 7

"All the gods of the Gentiles are devils" (Ps. 95).
"...Beware lest thou have a mind to imitate the abominations of those nations" (Dt. 18:9).

Principle 4

"This (episcopal) dignity, in fact, depends immediately on God as to the power of orders, and on the Apostolic See as to the power of jurisdiction..." (*Deessemus Nos*, Pope Pius VI).

Our position must be:

> We refuse...to follow the Rome of neo-Modernist and neo-Protestant tendencies which became clearly manifest during the Second Vatican Council and, after the Council, in all the reforms which issued from it.[6]

And it is neo-Modernist tendencies that the Council is all about.[7]

But wasn't the Council infallible?

- Not by reason of the extraordinary magisterium, for it refused to define anything. Pope Paul VI himself, in an audience on January 12, 1966, said that it "had avoided proclaiming in an extraordinary manner dogmas affected by the mark of infallibility."[8]

- Nor by reason of the ordinary universal magisterium, because this is not a defining power, but one of passing on what was always believed. The "universality" in question is not just one of place (all bishops) but also of time (always) (cf. Vatican I and Principle 6).

- Nor even by reason of the simply authentic magisterium, because the object of all magisterium is the deposit of faith to be guarded sacredly and expounded faithfully (Vatican I, Dz. 1836), and not to adopt as Catholic doctrine the "best expressed values of two centuries of 'liberal culture,'" even if they are "purified."[9]

---

6 Declaration of Archbishop Lefebvre, Appendix I.

7 "...Pope John Paul II makes not Holy Scripture, but rather Assisi, the shibboleth for the current understanding of the Council." *Pope John Paul II's Theological Journey to the Prayer Meeting of Religions in Assisi: Part I*, p. 46 (Appendix II).

8 Cf. the declaration of the Theological Commission of Mar. 6, 1964, and repeated by the Council's General Secretary on Nov. 16, 1964: "In view of conciliar practice and the pastoral purpose of the present Council, this sacred Synod defines matters of faith or morals as binding on the Church only when the Synod itself openly declares so." It never did.

9 Cardinal Ratzinger, *Gesu*, Nov. 1984, p. 72. Cf. *Gaudium et Spes*, §§11, 44.

VII

But shouldn't we follow the Pope?

The question of our attitude towards the Pope is a delicate one, especially since there is much confusion amongst Catholics concerning this question. The last fifty years have made this question more important than usual since we have witnessed the introduction of various theories and practices, often by the Popes themselves, that run counter to the perennial teaching of the Catholic Church. It behooves us then to look at the principles involved in this case:

First, there is no doubt that we believe all the dogmas of the Church, especially those concerning the office of the Papacy:

A) That it was divinely founded:

Thou art Peter; and upon this rock I will build my church, and the gates of hell shall not prevail against it. And I will give to thee the keys of the kingdom of heaven. And whatsoever thou shalt bind upon earth, it shall be bound also in heaven: and whatsoever thou shalt loose upon earth, it shall be loosed also in heaven. (Mt. 16:18-9)

B) That the Bishop of Rome has a primacy no other bishop has:

We point to the tradition of that very great and very ancient and universally known Church, which was founded and established at Rome, by the two most glorious Apostles, Peter and Paul: we point I say, to the tradition which this Church has from the Apostles, and to her faith proclaimed to men which comes down to our time through the succession of her bishops, and so we put to shame...all who assemble in unauthorized meetings. For with this Church, because of its superior authority, every Church must agree—that is the faithful everywhere—in communion with which Church the tradition of the Apostles has been always preserved by those who are everywhere. (St. Irenaeus, *Against Heresies*, III, 3:2.)

C) That the Pope is infallible under certain conditions:

The Roman Pontiff, when he speaks *ex cathedra*—that is, when in the exercise of his office as pastor and teacher of all Christians he defines, by virtue of his supreme Apostolic authority, a doctrine of faith or morals to be held by the whole Church—is, by reason of the Divine assistance promised to him in blessed Peter, possessed of that infallibility with which the Divine Redeemer wished His Church to be endowed in defining doctrines of faith and morals; and consequently that such definitions of the Roman Pontiff are irreformable of their own nature and not by reason of the Church's consent. (First Vatican Council, Dz. 1839)

There seem to be two errors common in these turbulent times. The first temptation is to presume to judge the Holy Father of being a formal heretic, a situation which would, according to them, cause the apparent Pope to be an anti-Pope, possessing no true jurisdiction. Although this has been put forward as a theoretical possibility by some theologians[1] historically, such a theory[2] cannot explain what happens to such doctrines as the visibility of the Church, or Christ's promise to be with His Church until the end of time. Such a simplistic notion is actually based on the same premise as the opposite temptation: that the Pope is actually protected by an extended infallibility which cannot account for any error.

The opposite error is far more common and assumes that whatever the Pope does or teaches is correct. This is perhaps understandable since, in normal times, this is in actuality what happens. But one must distinguish: history is replete with examples of Popes who taught or did things which were not proper. As an example, Pope Liberius signed some form of a semi-Arian document, and Pope John XXII temporarily taught that the souls of the saved do not see God until after the Final Judgment. Some Renaissance popes led lives of dubious morality. In all these cases, though wrong, papal infallibility was not involved.

The Pope is infallible primarily in matters of faith and morals, and secondarily in matters of discipline (legislation for the Universal Church, canonizations, *etc.*) to the extent that these involve faith and morals (cf. Principle 4), and then only when imposing for all time a definitive teaching. Indeed, if the Pope had some form of personal infallibility with regard to his ordinary teaching, there would be no need for a definition of its limits.

"Infallible" means immutable and irreformable (Principle 6), but, the hallmark of the conciliar Popes, like the Modernists, is a spirit of evolution. To what extent can such minds want irreformably to define or absolutely to impose? Cf. *QUESTION 15*, n. 3.

---

[1] By such men as Cajetan, St. Robert Bellarmine, and John of St. Thomas.
[2] There are different levels of theological certainty. Among these levels we might count revealed dogmas, which all Catholics must believe; teachings proximate to the Faith, which, though not defined, are generally regarded as true, and theological opinions, which the Church has not definitively settled and about which theologians disagree.

How then are we to judge him?

- First, it must be understood that it is a duty and necessity to pray for the Holy Father and his intentions.[3] As St. Clement Mary Hofbauer says: "A Christian who does not pray for the Pope is like a child who does not pray for his father."

- It is not for us to judge his culpability in the destruction of the Church. Only God can so judge him.

- Nor is it for us to judge him juridically—the Pope has no superior on earth—or to declare unquestionably null all his acts.

- We must thus make a judgment of his words and actions inasmuch as they affect our eternal salvation, as our Savior said:

Beware of false prophets who come to you in the clothing of sheep, but inwardly they are ravening wolves. By their fruits you shall know them (Mt. 7:15).

We are not to co-operate blindly in the destruction of the Church by tolerating the implementation of a new religion or by not doing what we can to defend the Catholic faith. Archbishop Lefebvre was surely our model here:

No authority, not even the highest in the hierarchy, can compel us to abandon or to diminish our Catholic Faith, so clearly expressed and professed by the Church's Magisterium for nineteen centuries.

"Friends," said St. Paul, "though it were we ourselves, though it were an angel from heaven that should preach to you a gospel other than the gospel we have preached to you, a curse upon him" (Gal. 1:8).

That is why, without any rebellion, bitterness, or resentment, we pursue our work of priestly formation under the guidance of the never-changing Magisterium, convinced as we are that we cannot possibly render a greater service to the Holy Catholic Church, to the Sovereign Pontiff, and to posterity.

---

[3] It should be noted that we do not speak primarily of the Pope's personal, subjective intentions. The six objective intentions of the Holy Father, traditionally understood, are: the exaltation of the Church, the propagation of the Faith, the extirpation of heresy, the conversion of sinners, concord between Christian princes, and the further welfare of the Christian people.

VIII

Shouldn't we accept the 1983 Code of Canon Law?

A code is a collection of laws, each one being an order of the competent authority: each canon in the 1917 Code of Canon Law was a law of Benedict XV, and each canon in the 1983 Code of Canon Law (commonly called the "New Code") is a law of Pope John Paul II.

For Pope John Paul II, the purpose of the 1983 Code of Canon Law is the expression of the Second Vatican Council's new ecclesiology (*i.e.*, the new understanding that the Church has of her nature and mission) in canonical language, and it must be understood always in the light of conciliar teaching.[1]

But that particular Council adulterated Catholic teaching.

---

[1] *Sacrae Disciplinae Leges*, Jan. 25, 1983.

We must, therefore, suspect the new legislation of codifying the same errors and so be ready not to accept all its "laws,"[2] but only those which do not evidently compromise Catholic teaching on faith or morals.

For the most part, we may regret the loss of clarity, precision, and integrity the 1917 Code of Canon Law had, but that is insufficient reason to reject these canons.

There are a few novelties, though, which must be rejected:

- Canon 844, §4 allows the administration of penance, anointing of the sick, and even holy Communion to non-Catholics who manifest "Catholic faith" (vs. Principle 7) in these sacraments. This used to be considered a *mortal sin* and was gravely forbidden (1917 Code of Canon Law, canon 731, §21) because it implicitly denies the dogma, "Outside the Church, no salvation" (Principle 2). This is an inadmissible surrender to modernist ecumenism.

- Canon 1055, §1 no longer defines marriage by its primary end, the procreation of children, but mentions this only after a secondary end, the good of the spouses. And this latter, as we can see in light of annulments now given, has become the *essence* of marriage[3]: the partners give each other their whole selves (and not just "the exclusive and perpetual right over the body of the partner as regards the acts capable in themselves of generating offspring," 1917 Code of Canon Law, canon 1081, §2) for their self-fulfillment in wedlock (canon 1057, §2). There is considered to be no marriage where one spouse cannot provide the other this help (canon 1095, §§2 and 3, canon 1098, *etc.*; cf. canon 1063, §4). Whence today's annulments fiasco: In the United States, for example, there were 338 annulments granted in 1968; there were 59,030 in 1992. Hence grave doubts are to be

---

[2] Cf. Principle 9.
[3] vs. Principles 5 and 6.

held concerning the annulments issued by *Novus Ordo* Tribunals.

- Canon 336 codifies the collegiality of Vatican II. The "college of Bishops," a twentieth-century invention, is now made a permanent subject, together with the Pope, of supreme and full power over the Universal Church. A bishop, moreover, participates in this universal jurisdiction by the mere fact of his consecration (cf. canon 375, §2).[4] This collegiality tampers with the divine constitution of the Church, derogates from the Pope's powers, and hampers his government of the Church (and that of the bishops in their dioceses). "Episcopal Conferences" now assume authority, which thus becomes impersonal and unanswerable.

These are but the most grave deficiencies; other defective points include the following:

- mixed marriages (canons 1125, 1127)

- diminution in censures (excommunication of Freemasons, *etc.*)

- The teaching of St. Thomas Aquinas is no longer strictly enjoined in seminaries (canons 251 ff.).

- General absolutions are more readily available (canons 961-963, *etc.*).

In passing, it is interesting to note that for Pope John Paul II the 1983 Code of Canon Law has less weight than a conciliar constitution.

---

[4] This becomes all the more disconcerting when one considers the recognition now given by the Vatican to the Orthodox Bishops. Cf. Pope Paul VI: "It is on the heads of the Churches, of their hierarchy, that the obligation rests to guide the Churches along the way that leads to full communion again. They ought to do this by recognizing and respecting each other as pastors of that part of the flock of Christ entrusted to them..." (Quoted at Balamand, by the Joint International Commission for the Theological Dialogue between the Roman Catholic Church and the Orthodox Church, Final Statement §18, cf. §14; *Ut Unum Sint,* §§50-63).

IX

Do traditional priests have jurisdiction?

In virtue of his ordination, a priest can bless all things and even consecrate bread and wine in such wise that they become the very Body and Blood of Our Lord Jesus Christ. But whenever in his ministry he has to deal authoritatively with people, he needs, over and above the power of Orders, that of *Jurisdiction*, which empowers him to judge and rule his flock. Jurisdiction is, moreover, necessary for the validity itself of the sacraments of penance and matrimony.

Now, the sacraments were given by Our Lord as the ordinary and principal means of salvation and sanctification. The Church, therefore, whose supreme law is the salvation of souls (1983 Code of Canon Law, canon 1752), wants the ready availability of these sacraments, and especially penance (canon 968). The Church wants priests (canon 1026) and empowers them liberally to hear confessions (canon 967, §2). This jurisdiction to hear confessions is to be revoked only for a grave reason (canon 974, §1).

Jurisdiction is ordinarily given by mandate from the Pope or diocesan bishop, or perhaps delegated by the parish priest. The priests of the Society of Saint Pius X do not have jurisdiction in this way. Extraordinarily, however, the Church supplies jurisdiction without passing by the constituted authorities. This is foreseen in the 1983 Code of Canon Law:

- when the faithful think the priest has a jurisdiction which he does not have (canon 144) [common error],

- when there is a probable and positive doubt that the priest has jurisdiction (canon 144),

- when a priest inadvertently continues to hear confessions once his faculties have expired (canon 142, §2), and

- when the penitent is in danger of death (and then even if the priest is laicized or an apostate, even though a Catholic priest is at hand) (canons 976, 1335).

Therefore, the Church, wanting the ready availability of penance, extraordinarily supplies jurisdiction in view of the needs of her children, and it is granted all the more liberally the greater their need.

Now, the nature of the present crisis in the Church is such that the faithful can on good grounds feel it a moral impossibility to approach priests having ordinary jurisdiction. And so, whenever the faithful need the graces of penance and want to receive them from priests whose judgment and advice they can trust, **they can do so**, even if the priests do not ordinarily have jurisdiction. Even a suspended priest can do this for the faithful who ask "for any just cause whatsoever" (canon 1335). This is even more the case if a faithful Catholic can foresee his being deprived of the true sacrament of penance from priests with ordinary jurisdiction until he dies. Only God knows when this crisis will end.

The extraordinary form for marriages is foreseen in canon 1116, §1. If the couple cannot approach their parish priest "without serious inconvenience"—and they may consider as such his insistence on having the *Novus Ordo Missae* for the wedding, or their apprehensions concerning his moral teaching in marriage instructions—and if they foresee these circumstances to last for at least a month, then they can marry before witnesses alone, and another priest (*e.g.*, of the Society of Saint Pius X) if possible (canon 1116, §2).

Even if one were to consider the above arguments as only probable, then jurisdiction would still be certainly supplied by the Church (canon 144). And so we must answer affirmatively. Traditional priests do have a jurisdiction that is neither territorial nor personal but supplied in view of the needs of the faithful.

X

May we attend the Masses offered under the provisions of Summorum Pontificum?

The Apostolic Letter Motu Proprio *Summorum Pontificum* has changed the juridical situation of the Mass. Until recently, the traditional Mass was presented as being prohibited and allowed only under an indult, that is, a special, exceptional permission joined with special conditions. The conditions attached to the celebration of the traditional Mass under the Indult were twofold: the recognition of the orthodoxy and legitimacy of the New Mass and the acceptance of the Second Vatican Council's decisions and reforms.

Pope Benedict XVI changed the juridical situation of the Mass by stating that the traditional Mass was never abrogated. Thanks to this statement, the Mass has been re-established as a universal law of the Church and can no longer be considered as prohibited or even as an exception. The expression "extraordinary form" used in the Motu Proprio is misleading.

Nevertheless, the practical situation of the Mass, due to the attitude of the majority of the bishops, has hardly changed from the previous state. Practically speaking, the bishops continue to limit the celebration of the traditional Mass by requiring priests and the faithful to apply for a permission that is no longer necessary, oftentimes in addition to other arbitrary conditions.

In other words, for the time being, there is in general hardly a difference from the previous situation with the Indult Mass, though in certain particular places there might be a better treatment for the Mass, the priests, and the faithful. This obliges us to invite the faithful to exercise the same prudence as before about attending the Indult Mass.

We hope that this situation will gradually change and that the reasons which oblige us today to be very restrictive will little by little disappear, in a process of gradually recovering the reality of the sacrifice, the reality of the priesthood and of the whole Christian spirit. But for now this is only a wish and a dream, apart from some exceptions.

Here is a summary of the dangers to which the faithful might easily be exposed by imprudently attending the traditional Mass celebrated today under said circumstances: the teaching of the Faith can still be defective, the priest might be ill-prepared for the pre-conciliar liturgy, the risk of a mixing of the new and old rite remains, and there is the danger of a confusion which could be very misleading.

In doubt, the faithful should ask their pastors for advice.

XI

Wasn't Archbishop Lefebvre excommunicated for consecrating bishops unlawfully?

June 29, 1987

Archbishop Lefebvre, experiencing failing health and seeing no other way of assuring the continued ordination of truly Catholic priests, decided to consecrate bishops and announced that, if necessary, he will do so even without the Pope's permission.

June 17, 1988

Cardinal Gantin, Prefect of the Congregation for Bishops, officially warned the Archbishop that, in virtue of canon 1382 (1983 Code of Canon Law), he and the bishops consecrated by him would be excommunicated for proceeding without pontifical mandate and thereby infringing the laws of sacred discipline.

June 30, 1988

Archbishop Lefebvre, together with Bishop de Castro Mayer, consecrated four bishops.

July 1, 1988

Cardinal Gantin declared the threatened excommunication (according to canon 1382) to have been incurred. He also called the consecrations a schismatic act and declared the corresponding excommunication (canon 1364, §1), as well as threatening anyone supporting the consecrations with excommunication because of "schism."

July 2, 1988

In the Apostolic Letter *Ecclesia Dei Adflicta*, the Pope repeated Cardinal Gantin's accusation of schismatic mentality and threatened generalized excommunications. (See *QUESTION 12*.)

2008

Bishop Fellay, at Lourdes in October, asked the faithful to offer a new Rosary Crusade for the intention of the lifting of the excommunication.

2009

On January 24, 2009, a letter from the Congregation of Bishops, signed by Cardinal Re, was released, stating that the Holy Father had decided to remit the ecclesiastical penalties of 1988. The status of the SSPX in the eyes of Rome is now vague, but what is clear is that they will no longer labor under the stigma of excommunication.

Now, the excommunication warned of on June 17, 1988, for abuse of episcopal powers (canon 1382), was not incurred because:

1) A person who violates a law out of necessity[1] is not subject to a penalty (1983 Code of Canon Law, canon 1323, no. 4), even if there is no state of necessity[2]:

- if one inculpably thought there was, he would not incur the penalty (canon 1323, no. 7),

- and if one culpably thought there was, he would still incur no automatic penalties[3] (canon 1324, §3; §1, no. 8).

2) No penalty is ever incurred without committing a subjective mortal sin (canons 1321, §1, 1323, no. 7). Now, Archbishop Lefebvre made it amply clear that he was bound in conscience to do what he could do to continue the Catholic priesthood and that he was obeying God in going ahead with the consecrations.[4] Hence, even if he had been wrong, there would be no subjective sin.

3) Most importantly, positive law is at the service of the natural and eternal law, and ecclesiastical law is at that of the divine law (Principle 8). No "authority,"[5] can force a bishop to compromise in his teaching of Catholic faith or administering of

---

[1] "The state of necessity, as it is explained by jurists, is a state in which the necessary goods for natural or supernatural life are so threatened that one is morally compelled to break the law in order to save them." *Is Tradition Excommunicated?* p. 26 (Appendix II).

[2] And yet objectively there is. Cf. *Is Tradition Excommunicated?* pp. 27-36 (Appendix II).

[3] Excommunication for unlawful consecrations (canon 1382) or schism (canon 1364) are of this kind.

[4] Cf. the Sermon of June 30, 1988, *Archbishop Lefebvre and the Vatican,* p. 136 (Appendix II).

[5] Principle 9.

Catholic sacraments. No "law" can force him to co-operate in the destruction of the Church. With Rome giving no guarantee of preserving Catholic Tradition, Archbishop Lefebvre had to do what he could with his God-given episcopal powers to guarantee its preservation. It was his duty as a bishop.

4) The Church's approving the Society of Saint Pius X (*QUESTION 2*) allows it what it needs for its own preservation. This includes the service of bishops who will guarantee to maintain Catholic tradition.

XII

Isn't the Society of St. Pius X schismatic?

Was Archbishop Lefebvre (along with his co-consecrator and the four bishops whom he consecrated) excommunicated also for having done a "schismatic act"?[1] No. The first argument for this question has been given (QUESTION 11, No. 1).

What, moreover, constitutes a schismatic act? Not the mere deed of consecrating bishops without pontifical mandate. The 1983 Code of Canon Law itself lists this offense under Title 3 (abuse of ecclesiastical powers) and not under Title 1 (offenses against religion and the unity of the Church) of its penal section (Book 6).

Nor would it be a "schismatic act" to consecrate against the express wish of the Holy Father. That could amount to disobedience at

---

[1] As well as for consecrating without a pontifical mandate, QUESTION 11.

most.[2] But disobedience does not amount to schism; schism requires that one not recognize the authority of the pope to command; disobedience consists in not obeying a command, whilst still acknowledging the authority of the one commanding. "The child who says 'I won't!' to his mother does not deny that she is his mother."[3]

Now, Archbishop Lefebvre always recognized the Pope's authority (proved by his consultations with Rome for a solution to the current problems) and so does the Society of Saint Pius X. (See, for example, its support for Pope John Paul's *Ordinatio Sacerdotalis* against women priests.)

Consecrating a bishop without pontifical mandate would be a schismatic act if one pretended to confer not just the fullness of the priesthood but also jurisdiction, a governing power over a particular flock. Only the Pope, who has universal jurisdiction over the whole Church, can appoint a pastor to a flock and empower him to govern it. But Archbishop Lefebvre never presumed to confer anything but the full priestly powers of Orders, and in no way did he grant any jurisdiction (which he himself did not have personally to give).

As for the faithful, threatened by Pope John Paul II himself with excommunication if they adhere formally to the schism (*Ecclesia Dei Adflicta*, July 2, 1988), do they indeed incur any excommunication for going to Society of Saint Pius X priests for the sacraments?

Not at all. The Society of Saint Pius X priests are neither excommunicated nor schismatics.[4] This being so, how could any of the faithful who approach them incur these penalties? Besides, "Excommunication is a penalty for those who commit certain crimes with full moral guilt, not a contagious disease!"[5]

---

[2] But there is no disobedience, cf. *An Open Letter to Confused Catholics*, pp. 129-136, (Appendix II). Cf. "The act of consecrating a bishop (without the Pope's permission) is not in itself a schismatic act," Cardinal Lara, President of the Pontifical Commission for the Authentic Interpretation of Canon Law, in *La Repubblica*, Oct. 7, 1988.

[3] Fr. Glover, in *Is Tradition Excommunicated?* p. 99 (Appendix II).

[4] *Is Tradition Excommunicated?* pp. 1-39 (Appendix II).

[5] Fr. Glover, *op. cit.*, p. 100.

On May 1, 1991, Bishop Ferrario of Hawaii "excommunicated" certain Catholics of his diocese for attending Masses celebrated by priests of the Society of Saint Pius X, and receiving a bishop of the Society of Saint Pius X to confer the sacrament of Confirmation. Cardinal Ratzinger, Prefect of the Congregation for the Doctrine of the Faith, overturned this decision:

> From the examination of the case...it did not result that the facts referred to in the above-mentioned decree, are formal schismatic acts in the strict sense, as they do not constitute the offense of schism; and therefore the Congregation holds that the Decree of May 1, 1991, lacks foundation and hence validity (June 28, 1993).

On February 8, 2007, Cardinal Hoyos in an interview stated: "Please accept that I reject the term 'ecumenism ad intra.' The bishops, priests and faithful of the Society of St. Pius X are not schismatics....The priests and faithful of the Society have not been excommunicated. They are not heretics."

It seems even Rome wishes to avoid using this term now.

XIII

What are we to think of the Fraternity of St. Peter?

Since the introduction of the new sacramental rites, Rome had allowed no Society or Congregation exclusive use of the older rites. Then on June 30, 1988, Archbishop Lefebvre consecrated four bishops to ensure the survival of the traditional priesthood and sacraments, and especially of the traditional Latin Mass. Suddenly, within two days, Pope John Paul II recognized[1] the "rightful aspirations" (for these things) of those who wouldn't support Archbishop Lefebvre's stance, and offered to give to them what he had always refused the Archbishop. A dozen or so priests of the Society of Saint Pius X accepted this "good will" and broke away to found the Fraternity of Saint Peter.

---

[1] *Ecclesia Dei Adflicta*, July 2, 1988.

The Fraternity of Saint Peter is founded upon more than questionable principles, for the following reasons:

(i) It accepts that the conciliar Church has the power:

- to take away the Mass of all time (for the *Novus Ordo Missae* is not another form of this, *QUESTION 5*),

- to grant it to those only who accept the same conciliar Church's novel orientations (in life, belief, structures),

- to declare non-Catholic those who deny this by word or deed,[2] and

- to profess itself in a certain way in communion with anyone calling himself "Christian," and yet to declare itself out of communion with Catholics whose sole crime is wanting to remain Catholic.[3]

(ii) In practice, the priests of the Fraternity of Saint Peter, having recourse to a *Novus Ordo* bishop willing to permit the traditional rites and willing to ordain their candidates, they are forced to abandon the fight against the new religion which is being installed:

- They reject the *Novus Ordo Missae* only because it is not their "spirituality" and claim the traditional Latin Mass only in virtue of their "charism" acknowledged them by the Pope.

- They seek to ingratiate themselves with the local bishops, praising them for the least sign of Catholic spirit and keeping quiet on their modernist deviations,[4] even though by doing so they end up encouraging them along their wrong path.

---

[2] An interpretation of "Everyone should be aware that formal adherence to the schism (of Archbishop Lefebvre) is a grave offense against God and carries the penalty of excommunication," *Ecclesia Dei Adflicta.*

[3] Vatican II, *e.g. Lumen Gentium* §15; *Unitatis Redintegratio* §3.

[4] Unless perhaps it is a question of a diocese where they have no hopes of starting up.

- Note, for example, the Fraternity of Saint Peter's whole-hearted acceptance of the Catechism of the Catholic Church (*QUESTION 14*), acceptance of *Novus Ordo* professors in their seminaries, and blanket acceptance of Vatican II's orthodoxy (*QUESTION 6*).

They are therefore conciliar Catholics and not traditional Catholics. This being so, attending their Mass is:

- accepting the compromise on which they are based,

- accepting the direction taken by the conciliar Church and the consequent destruction of the Catholic Faith and practices, and

- accepting, in particular, the lawfulness and doctrinal soundness of the *Novus Ordo Missae* and Vatican II.

That is why a Catholic ought not to attend their Masses.

XIV

What are we to think of the new Catechism of the Catholic Church?

This question illustrates the fundamental differences between the Society of Saint Pius X and the conciliar "traditionalists" or conservatives. These latter are often seen defending both the traditional Latin Mass and the "new" Catechism but not openly attacking either the *Novus Ordo Missae* or Vatican II. The Society of Saint Pius X on the other hand defends the traditional catechisms and therefore the traditional Latin Mass, and so attacks the *Novus Ordo Missae*, Vatican II and the "new" Catechism, all of which more or less undermine our unchangeable Catholic faith.

Conservatives defend the Catechism of the Catholic Church for its re-affirmation of teachings silenced or denied by outrightly modernist catechisms; the Society of Saint Pius X rejects it though because it is an attempt to formalize and propagate the teachings of Vatican II. Pope John Paul II agrees with this:

> The *Catechism* was also indispensable,[1] in order that all the richness of the teaching of the Church following the Second Vatican Council could be preserved in a new synthesis and be given a new direction.[2]

One need but consider the 806 citations from Vatican II, a number which amounts on average to one citation every three-and-a-half paragraphs throughout the 2,865 paragraphs of the Catechism.

In particular, the novelties of Vatican II appear in the following paragraphs:

- an infatuation with the dignity of man (§§225, 369, 1700, 1929...)
    1. such that we may hope for the salvation of all the baptized (§§1682 ff.),
    2. even non-Catholics (§818),
    3. or those who commit suicide (§2283),
    4. and of all the unbaptised, whether adults (§847),
    5. or infants (§1261);
    6. which is the basis of all rights (§§1738, 1930, 1935) including that of religious liberty (§§2106 ff.),
    7. and the motive of all morality (§§1706, 1881, 2354, 2402, 2407, *etc.*).

- a commitment to ecumenism (§§820 f., 1399, 1401) because all religions are instruments of salvation (§§819, 838-843, 2104),

- collegiality (§§879-885),

- over-emphasis on the priesthood of the faithful (§§873, 1547, 1140 ff., *etc.*).

---

[1] *I.e.*, as well as the 1983 Code of Canon Law.
[2] John Paul II, *Crossing the Threshold of Hope* (London: Jonathen Cape, 1994), p. 164.

Now, just as he who denies but one article of Faith loses the Faith (cf. Principle 7), so a teacher who errs on one point alone proves himself fallible and renders all he teaches questionable.

Just as the Second Vatican Council is not an authority to quote even where it propounds Catholic teaching (it does not do so infallibly and clearly), so this Catechism is not an authority of Catholic belief because of the modern deviations which it encompasses.

Those who defend this Catechism are supporting the innovations of Vatican II.

XV

What are we to think of the sedevacantists?

In the face of the scandal of a Pope who can sign *Dignitatis Humanae*, radically change the liturgy of the Mass, codify a new ecclesiology, or make himself the protagonist for an aberrant ecumenism, *etc.*, some have concluded that the last Popes cannot have been true Popes, or else that they have lost the pontificate because of such scandals. They refer to the discussions of the great Counter-Reformation theologians on the loss of the pontificate (through abdication, insanity, heresy, *etc.*) and argue thus:

- He who is not a member of the Church can't be its head.

- But a heretic is not a member of the Church.

- Now, Pope John XXIII, Pope Paul VI, Pope John Paul I and Pope John Paul II are heretics.

- Therefore, they are neither members nor head of the Church,

- and so all their acts are to be completely ignored.

But then again, the argument continues, the same scandals are true of all the world's diocesan bishops, who are also consequently non-members without authority; and the Catholic Church must be identified only with those who have not compromised the Faith and who refuse communion with these "popes" or "bishops." A minority of these will elect their own "pope."[1]

The argument's strength is in the real scandal of the conciliar authorities' impetus given to the Church's "new direction"; its weakness is in not being able to prove that any of these authorities are formal heretics.

- You are a "material" heretic without knowing it if you objectively contradict what God has said but through no fault of your own;

- you are a "formal" heretic if you do pertinaciously contradict what God has said, *i.e.* knowing that you're denying what God has said and wanting to do this anyway.

Now, the ordinary way for the Church to ascertain pertinacity and enforce the consequences of one's heresy by either excommunication and/or loss of office, is through authoritative monitions[2] to the delinquent which he spurns (1983 Code of Canon Law, canon 2314, §1). But nobody can authoritatively admonish the Pope (canon 1556), and the bishops can only be admonished by their superior, the Pope (canon 1557), who has not done so.

Therefore, pertinacity, and so formal heresy, cannot be proven.

---

[1] *E.g.*, the communities at Palmar de Troya, Spain, or St. Jovite, Canada.

[2] To have canonical force, they must come from one's superior (cf. canon 2233). The point is not only the crime but also its imputability must be notorious (canon 2195; 2197).

But could pertinacity not be presumed from the insistence of these Popes on the new ways, and this in the face of all tradition and its present-day witnesses? Perhaps; but not socially *i.e.*, as regards loss of office, *etc.*, which must not be presumed but proven, otherwise societies would collapse.

The argument does not prove its point, and becomes less probable when you consider that there are other explanations for the "material heretic" Pope (a)—(see below), and it becomes quite improbable when you consider its dangers (b) or consequences (c).

a) The liberal mindset of a Pope Paul VI or a Pope John Paul II can be an explanation of their wanting to be Catholics and their simultaneous betrayal in practice of Catholicism. They accept contradictions; with a subjective and evolutive mentality, this is to be expected.[3] But such a frame of mind can be convinced of heresy only by way of authority...

b) The Church is *indefectible* (Principle 3) not only in her faith and means of sanctification, but also in her monarchical constitution (Principle 4), comprising governing power *i.e.*, jurisdiction, hence Vatican I's profession that Peter will have *perpetual* successors.

Now, we can understand a break in the line of Popes from the death of one to the election of the next, and that it may drag on.

But is indefectibility preserved if there has been no Pope since 1962 or if there is no one with ordinary jurisdiction whom the sedevacantists can point out as such?

The Church is visible (Principle 3) and not just a society composed of those who are joined by interior bonds (state of grace, same

---

[3] A little example: "At the Second Vatican Council, the Catholic Church committed herself irrevocably to following the path of the ecumenical venture, thus heeding the Spirit of the Lord, who teaches people to interpret carefully the 'signs of the times'" (*Ut Unum Sint,* §3). If it is because of the "signs of the times" that the conciliar Church has launched herself into ecumenism, how are we to know that the venture will be irrevocable? What does a Pope John Paul II mean by such absolute terms?

faith...). A society is recognized and maintained as such by its authority (its efficient cause).

c) If the Church has not had a Pope since the days of Vatican II, then there are no more cardinals legitimately created. But then how is the Church to get a Pope again, as the current discipline grants only to cardinals the power to elect a Pope?

The Church could have ordained that non-cardinal "electors of the Pope" be capable of doing it, but we cannot go by any other way than the current discipline which ordains that cardinals elect him.

A few sedevacantists hold that he has been or will be directly designated by private revelation from heaven.

There are spiritual consequences of sedevacantism:

- Sedevacantism is a theological opinion, and not a certitude.

To treat it as a certitude leads to condemning with temerity traditional Catholics who disagree; and invariably it leads to one's recognizing no spiritual superiors on earth. Each becomes, in practice, his own little "pope," the rule of faith and orthodoxy, the judge of the validity of sacraments.[4] This being so, we ought not to associate with or receive the sacraments from them, most especially if they set up sedevacantism as a certitude which all have to accept.

---

[4] Consider the arguments from "Bishop" Vezelis, the Schuckardt movement, *etc.*: It is said that Cardinal Lienart, who ordained Archbishop Lefebvre a priest and consecrated him a bishop, was a Freemason, and so all his ordinations were invalid; and so we must consider invalid all the sacraments of those he ordained, and of those they ordained... In fact, whereas that Lienart was a Freemason is only an unproven allegation of one writer; and Church teaching is that we must accept as valid his sacraments anyway, if he used the correct external rite (unless he revealed a contrary internal intention, which he didn't). Moreover, Archbishop Lefebvre was consecrated by three bishops in 1947, which sacrament was therefore surely valid.

APPENDIX I

Declaration of Archbishop Lefebvre Ecône, November 21, 1974

We hold fast, with all our heart and with all our soul, to Catholic Rome, Guardian of the Catholic faith and of the traditions necessary to preserve this faith, to Eternal Rome, Mistress of wisdom and truth.

We refuse, on the other hand, and have always refused to follow the Rome of neo-Modernist and neo-Protestant tendencies which were clearly evident in the Second Vatican Council and, after the Council, in all the reforms which issued from it.

All these reforms, indeed, have contributed and are still contributing to the destruction of the Church, to the ruin of the priesthood, to the abolition of the Sacrifice of the Mass and of the sacraments, to the disappearance of religious life, to a naturalist and Teilhardian teaching in universities, seminaries and catechetics; a teaching derived from Liberalism and Protestantism, many times condemned by the solemn Magisterium of the Church.

No authority, not even the highest in the hierarchy, can force us to abandon or diminish our Catholic faith, so clearly expressed and professed by the Church's Magisterium for nineteen centuries.

"But though we," says St. Paul, "or an angel from heaven preach a gospel to you besides that which we have preached to you, let him be anathema" (Gal. 1:8).

Is it not this that the Holy Father is repeating to us today?[1] And if we can discern a certain contradiction in his words and deeds, as well as in those of the dicasteries, well we choose what was always taught and we turn a deaf ear to the novelties destroying the Church.

It is impossible to modify profoundly the *lex orandi* without modifying the *lex credendi*. To the *Novus Ordo Missae* correspond a new catechism, a new priesthood, new seminaries, a charismatic Pentecostal Church—all things opposed to orthodoxy and the perennial teaching of the Church.

This Reformation, born of Liberalism and Modernism, is poisoned through and through; it derives from heresy and ends in heresy, even if all its acts are not formally heretical. It is therefore impossible for any conscientious and faithful Catholic to espouse this Reformation or to submit to it in any way whatsoever.

The only attitude of faithfulness to the Church and Catholic doctrine, in view of our salvation, is a categorical refusal to accept this Reformation.

That is why, without any spirit of rebellion, bitterness or resentment, we pursue our work of forming priests, with the timeless Magisterium as our guide. We are persuaded that we can render no greater service to the Holy Catholic Church, to the Sovereign Pontiff and to posterity.

That is why we hold fast to all that has been believed and practiced in the faith, morals, liturgy, teaching of the catechism, formation of the priest and institution of the Church, by the Church of all time; to all these things as codified in those books which saw day before the Modernist influence of the Council. This we shall do until such time that the true light of Tradition dissipates the darkness obscuring the sky of Eternal Rome.

---

[1] A reference to Paul VI's "Credo of the People of God" (June 30, 1968).

By doing this, with the grace of God and the help of the Blessed Virgin Mary, and that of St. Joseph and St. Pius X, we are assured of remaining faithful to the Roman Catholic Church and to all the successors of Peter, and of being the *fideles dispensatores mysteriorum Domini Nostri Jesu Christi in Spiritu Sancto.*[2] Amen.

---

[2] "Faithful dispensers of the mysteries of Our Lord Jesus Christ in the Holy Ghost" (cf. I Cor. 4:1 ff.).

APPENDIX II

*Jubilee Sermon of Archbishop Lefebvre
On the Occasion of His Sacerdotal Jubilee
September 23, 1979*

My dear Brethren,

Allow me before beginning the few words which I would like to address to you on the occasion of this beautiful ceremony, to thank all those who have contributed to its magnificent success.

Personally, I had thought of celebrating my sacerdotal jubilee in a private, discreet manner at the altar which is the heart of Ecône, but the beloved clergy of St. Nicolas du Chardonnet and the beloved priests who surround me, invited me with such insistence to permit all those who desired to unite themselves in my thanksgiving and my prayer on the occasion of this sacerdotal jubilee, that I could not refuse and that is why we are gathered here today—so great in numbers, so diverse in origin—having come from America, from all European countries which are yet free. Here we are united for the occasion of this sacerdotal jubilee.

How then could I define this gathering, this manifestation, this ceremony? homage, a homage to your faith in the Catholic priesthood, and in the holy Catholic Mass. I truly believe that it is for this reason that you have come, in order to manifest your attachment to the Catholic Church and to the most beautiful treasure, to the most sublime gift which God has given to man: the priesthood, and the priesthood for sacrifice, for the Sacrifice of Our Lord continued upon our altars.

This is why you have come; this is why we are surrounded today by these beloved priests who have come from everywhere and many more would have come were it not a Sunday, for they are held, by their obligations to celebrate Holy Mass in their parishes, and they have told us so.

I would like to trace, if you will permit me, some scenes to which I have been a witness during the course of this half century, in order to show more clearly the importance which the Mass of the Catholic Church holds in our life, in the life of a priest, in the life of a bishop, and in the life of the Church.

As a young seminarian at Santa Chiara, the French Seminary in Rome, they used to teach us attachment to liturgical ceremonies. I had, during that time, the privilege of being a *ceremoniaire,* that which we call a "master of ceremonies," having been preceded no less in this office by His Grace Msgr. Lebrune, the former Bishop of Autun, and by His Grace Msgr. Ancel, who is still the Auxiliary Bishop of Lyons. I was therefore a master of ceremonies under the direction of the beloved Fr. Haegy, known for his profound knowledge of the liturgy. We loved to prepare the altar; we loved to prepare the ceremonies and we were already imbued with the spirit of the feast the eve of the day when a great ceremony was to take place upon our altars. We understood therefore, as young seminarians, to love the altar.

Domine, dilexi decorem domus tuae et gloriam habitionis tuae. This is the verse which we recite during the Lavabo at the altar: "Lord I have loved Thy house and the glory of Thy dwelling."

This is what they taught us at the French Seminary in Rome under the direction of the dear and Reverend Fr. Le Floch, a well loved Father, who taught us to see clearly the events of the time through his commentaries on the encyclicals of the popes.

I was ordained a priest in the Chapel of the Sacred Heart de la rue Royale in Lille on September 21, 1929, by the then Archbishop Liénart. I left shortly afterwards—two years afterwards—for the missions to join my brother who was already there in Gabon. There I began to learn what the Mass truly is.

Certainly I knew by the studies which we had done, what this great mystery of our Faith was, but I had not yet understood its entire value, efficacy and depth. This I learned day by day, year by year, in Africa, and particularly in Gabon, where I spent 13 years of my missionary life, first at the seminary and then in the bush among the Africans, with the natives.

There I saw—yes, I saw—what the grace of the Holy Mass could do. I saw it in the holy souls of some of our catechists. I saw it in those pagan souls transformed by the grace of baptism, transformed by assistance at Holy Mass, and by the Holy Eucharist. These souls understood the mystery of the Sacrifice of the Cross and united themselves to Our Lord Jesus Christ in the sufferings of His Cross, offering their sacrifices and their sufferings with Our Lord Jesus Christ, and living as Christians.

I can cite names: Paul Ossima of Ndjolé, Eugene Ndonc of Lambaréné, Marcel Mable of Donguila, and I will continue with a name from Senegal, Mr. Forster, Treasurer-Paymaster in Senegal, chosen for this delicate and important function by his peers and even by the Moslems due to his honesty and integrity. These are some of the men produced by the grace of the Mass. They assisted at the Mass daily, communicating with great fervor and they have become models and the light of those about them. This is just to list a few without counting the many Christians transformed by this grace.

I was able to see these pagan villages become Christian, being transformed not only, I would say, spiritually and supernaturally, but also being transformed physically, socially, economically and politically. Because these people—pagans that they were—became cognizant of the necessity of fulfilling their duties, in spite of trials, in spite of the sacrifices of maintaining their commitments, particularly their commitment in marriage. Then the village began to be transformed little by little under the influence of grace, under the influence of the grace of the Holy Sacrifice of the Mass. Soon all the villages were wanting to have one of the Fathers visit them. Oh, the visit of a missionary! They waited impatiently to assist at the Holy Mass in order to be able to confess their sins and then to receive Holy Communion.

Some of these souls also consecrated themselves to God: nuns, priests, brothers, giving themselves to God, consecrating themselves to God. There you have the fruit of the Holy Mass.

Why did all this happen?

It is necessary that we study somewhat the profound motive of this transformation: sacrifice.

The notion of sacrifice is a profoundly Christian and a profoundly Catholic notion. Our life cannot be spent without sacrifice, since Our Lord Jesus Christ, God Himself, willed to take a body like our own and say to us: "Follow Me, take up thy cross and follow Me if thou wilt be saved." And He has given us the example of His death upon the Cross; He has shed His Blood. Would we then dare—we, His miserable creatures, sinners that we are—not to follow Our Lord in pursuit of His Sacrifice, in pursuit of His Cross?

There is the entire mystery of Christian civilization. There is that which is the root of Christian civilization: the comprehension of sacrifice in one's life, in daily life, the understanding of Christian suffering, no longer considering suffering as an evil, as an unbearable sorrow, but sharing one's sufferings and one's sickness with the sufferings of Our Lord Jesus Christ, in looking upon His Cross, in assisting at the Holy Mass, which is the continuation of the Passion of Our Lord upon Calvary.

Once understood, suffering becomes a joy and a treasure because these sufferings, if united to those of Our Lord, if united to those of all the martyrs, of all Catholics, of all the faithful who suffer in this world, if, united to the Cross of Our Lord, they, then become an inexpressible treasure, a treasure unutterable, and achieve an extraordinary capacity for the conversion of other souls and the salvation of our own. Many holy souls, Christians, have even desired to suffer in order to unite themselves more closely to the Cross of Our Lord Jesus Christ. There you have Christian civilization:

Blessed are those who suffer for righteousness sake.
Blessed are the poor.
Blessed are the meek.
Blessed are the merciful.
Blessed are the peace-makers.

These are the teachings of the Cross; it is this that Our Lord Jesus Christ teaches us by His Cross.

This Christian civilization, penetrating to the depths of nations only recently pagan, has transformed them, and impelled them to desire and thus to choose Catholic heads of state. I myself have known and aided the leaders of these Catholic countries. Their Catholic peoples desired to have Catholic leaders so that even their governments and all the laws of their land might be submissive to the laws of Our Lord Jesus Christ and to the Ten Commandments.

If, in the past, France—said to be Catholic—had truly fulfilled the role of a Catholic power, she would have supported these colonized lands in their new-found Faith. Had she done so, their lands would not now be menaced by Communism, and Africa would not be what it is today. The fault does not so much lie with the Africans them-selves as with the colonial powers, which did not understand how to avail themselves of this Christian faith which had rooted itself among the African peoples. With a proper understanding they would have been able to exercise a brotherly influence among these nations by helping them to keep the Faith and exclude Communism.

If we look back through history, we see immediately that what I have been speaking of took place in bur own countries in the first centuries after Constantine. For we too, are, in our origins, converts. Our ancestors were converted, our kings were converted, and down through the centuries they offered their nations to Our Lord Jesus Christ, and they submitted their countries to the Cross of Jesus. They willed too that Mary should be the Queen of their lands.

One can read the admirable writings of St. Edward, King of England, of St. Louis, King of France, of the Holy Roman Emperor St. Henry, of St. Elizabeth of Hungary, and of all the saints who were at the head of our Catholic nations and who thus helped to make Christianity.

What faith they had in the Holy Mass! King St. Louis of France served two Masses every day. If he was traveling and happened to hear church bells ringing to announce the consecration, he would dismount to adore on bended knee the miracle being performed at that moment. There indeed was Catholic civilization! How far from such faith we are now, how far indeed!

There is another event which we are bound to mention after these pictures of Christian civilization in Africa, and in our own history, that of France particularly. A recent event, an event in the life of the Church, and an important event: the Second Vatican Council. We are obliged to declare that the enemies of the Church knew very well, perhaps better than we, what the value of just one Mass is. There was a poem once written on this subject in which one finds words attributed to Satan showing how he trembles each time a Mass, a true Catholic Mass, is celebrated because he is thus reminded of the memory of the Cross, and he knows well that it was by the Cross that he was vanquished. The enemies of the Church who perform sacrilegious masses in the well-known sects, and the Communists, too, know what value is to be had from one Mass, one true Catholic Mass.

I was recently told that in Poland the Communist Party through their "Inspectors of Religion," keep under surveillance those priests in Poland who say the Old Mass but leave alone those who say the New. They persecute those who say the Old Mass, the Mass of All Time. A foreign priest visiting Poland may say what Mass he pleases in order to give the impression of freedom, but the Polish priests who decide to hold firm to Tradition are persecuted.

I read recently a document about the PAX movement which was communicated to us in June of 1963 in the name of Cardinal Wyszynski. This document told us:

> You think we have freedom, you are made to think that we have it, and it is the priests affiliated with PAX, who are friends of the Communist government, who spread these ideas abroad because they are propagandists for the government, as is even the progressive French press. But it is not true; we are not free.

Cardinal Wyszynski gave precise details. He said that in the youth camps organized by the Communists the children were kept behind barbed wire on Sundays to keep them from going to Mass. He told, too, how vacation hideaways organized by the Catholic priests were surveilled from helicopters to see if the youth were going to Mass. Why, why this need to spy upon children on their way to Mass? Because they know that the Mass is absolutely anti-Communist and, how indeed could it be otherwise? For what is Communism if not "all for the Party and all for the Revolution"? The Mass, on the other hand, is "all for God." Not at all the same thing is it?

All for God! This is the Catholic Mass, opposed as it is to the program of the Party, which is a Satanic program.

You know well that we are all tested, that we are all beset with difficulties in our lives, in our earthly existence. We all have the need to know why we suffer, why these trials and sorrows, why these Catholics are lying sick in their beds; the hospitals are full of sick people. Why?

The Christian responds: to unite my sufferings to those of Our Lord on the altar, to unite them on the altar and through that act to participate in the work of redemption, to merit for myself and for other souls the joy of heaven.

Now it was during the Council that the enemies of the Church infiltrated Her, and their first objective was to demolish and destroy the Mass insofar as they could. You can read the books of Michael Davies, an English Catholic, who has written magnificent works which demonstrate how the liturgical reform of Vatican II closely resembles that produced under Cranmer at the birth of English Protestantism. If one reads the history of that liturgical transformation, made also by Luther, one sees that now it is exactly the same procedure which is being slowly followed and to all appearances, still apparently good and Catholic. But it is just that character of the Mass which is sacrificial and redemptive of sin, through the Blood of Our Lord Jesus Christ, which they have removed. They have made of the Mass a simple assembly, one among others, merely presided over by the priest. That is not the Mass!

It is not surprising that the Cross no longer triumphs, because the sacrifice no longer triumphs. It is not surprising that men think no longer of anything but raising their standard of living, that they seek only money, riches, pleasures, comfort, and the easy ways of this world. They have lost the sense of sacrifice.

What does it remain for us to do, my dear brethren, if in this manner we deepen our understanding of the great mystery which is the Mass? Well, I think I can say what we should have: a *crusade!* A crusade supported by the Holy Sacrifice of the Mass, by the Blood of Our Lord Jesus Christ, by that invincible rock, that inexhaustible source of grace, the Holy Sacrifice of the Mass.

This we see every day. You are here because you love the Holy Sacrifice of the Mass. And these young seminarians who are in the seminary in Ecône, the United States, and Germany—why do they come into our seminaries? For the Holy Mass, for the Holy Mass of All Time which is the source of grace, the source of the Holy Ghost, the source of Christian civilization; that is the reason for the priest.

It is necessary that we undertake a crusade, a crusade which is based precisely upon these notions of immutability, of sacrifice, in order to recreate Christianity, to reestablish a Christendom such as the Church desires, such as She has always done, with the same principles, the same Sacrifice of the Mass, the same sacraments, the same catechism, the same Holy Scripture. We must recreate this Christendom! It is to you, my dear brethren, you who are the salt of the earth and the light of the world, that our Lord Jesus Christ addressed Himself in saying: "Do not lose the fruit of My Blood, do not abandon My Calvary, do not abandon My Sacrifice." And the Virgin Mary who stands beneath the Cross, tells you the same thing as well. She, whose heart is pierced, full of sufferings and sorrow, yet at the same time filled with the joy of uniting herself to the Sacrifice of her Divine Son; she says to you as well: "Let us be Christians; let us be Catholics."

Let us not be borne away by all these worldly ideas, by all these currents of thought which are in the world, and which draw us to sin and to hell. If we want to go to heaven we must follow Our Lord Jesus Christ. We must carry our cross and follow Our Lord Jesus Christ, imitating Him in His Cross, in His suffering, in His Sacrifice.

Thus I ask the youth, the young people who are here in this hall, to ask us to explain to them these things that are so beautiful and so great, so as to choose their vocations, whatever be the calling that they may elect—be they priests or religious men and women, or married by the Sacrament of Matrimony, and, therefore, in the Cross of Jesus Christ, and in the Blood of Jesus Christ, married in the grace of Our Lord Jesus Christ. Let them comprehend the greatness of matrimony, and let them prepare themselves worthily for it—by purity and chastity, by prayer and reflection. Let them not be carried away by all the passions which engulf the world. Thus let this be the crusade of the young who must aspire to the true ideal.

Let it be as well a crusade for Christian families. You Christian families who are here, consecrate yourselves to the Heart of Jesus, to the Eucharistic Heart of Jesus and to the Immaculate Heart of

Mary. Oh, pray together in the family! I know that many of those among you already do so, but may there always be more and more of you who do so with fervor. Let Our Lord truly reign in your homes!

Cast away, I beg of you, anything which impedes children from entering your family. There is no greater gift that the Good God can bestow upon your hearths than to have many children. Have big families. It is the glory of the Catholic Church—the large family! It has been so in Canada, it has been so in Holland, it has been so in Switzerland and it has been so in France—everywhere the large family was the joy and prosperity of the Church. There are that many more chosen souls for heaven! Therefore do not limit, I beg you, the gifts of God; do not listen to these abominable slogans which destroy the family, which ruin health, which ruin the household, and provoke divorce.

And I wish that, in these troubled times, in this degenerate urban atmosphere in which we are living, that you return to the land whenever possible. The land is healthy; the land teaches one to know God; the land draws one to God; it calms temperaments, characters, and encourages the children to work.

And if it is necessary, yes, you yourselves will make the school for your children. If the schools should corrupt your children, what are you going to do? Deliver them to the corrupters? To those who teach these abominable sexual practices in the schools? To the so-called "Catholic" schools run by religious men and women where they simply teach sin? In reality that is what they are teaching to the children: they corrupt them from their tenderest youth. Are you to put up with that? It is inconceivable! Rather that your children be poor—that they be removed from this apparent science that the world possesses—but that they be good children, Christian children, Catholic children, who love their holy religion, who love to pray, and who love to work; children who love the earth which the Good God has made.

Finally, a crusade as well for heads of families. You who are the head of your household, you have a grave responsibility in your countries. You do not have the right to let your country be invaded by Socialism and Communism! You do not have the right, or else you are no longer Catholic! You must fight at the time of elections in order that you may have Catholic mayors, Catholic deputies, so that France finally may become Catholic again. That is not mere politics, that is to wage a good, campaign, a campaign such as was waged by the saints, such as was waged the popes who opposed Attila, such as was waged by St. Remy who converted Clovis, such as was waged by Joan of Arc who saved France from Protestantism. If Joan of Arc had not been raised up in France we would all be Protestants! It was in order to keep France Catholic that Our Lord raised up Joan of Arc, that child of seventeen years, who drove the English out of France. That, too, is waging a political campaign.

Surely then this is the sort of politics which we desire: the politics of the royalty of Our Lord Jesus Christ. Just a few moments ago you were heard to chant: *Christus vincit, Christus regnat, Christus imperat.* Are these but words, mere lyrics, mere chants? No! It is necessary that they be a reality. You heads of the family, you are the ones responsible for such realization, both for your children and for the generations which are to come. Thus you should organize yourselves now, conduct meetings and hear yourselves out, with the object that France become once again Christian, once again Catholic, It is not impossible, otherwise one would have to say that the grace of the Holy Sacrifice of the Mass is no longer grace, that God is no longer God, that Our Lord Jesus Christ is no longer Our Lord Jesus Christ. One must have confidence in the grace of Our Lord Who is all-powerful. I have seen this grace at work in Africa. There is no reason why it will not work as well here in these countries. This is the message I wanted to tell you today.

And you, dear priests, who hear me now, you too must make a profound sacerdotal union to spread this crusade, to animate this crusade in order that Jesus reign, that Our, Lord reign. And to do that you must be holy. You must seek after sanctity and manifest it to others, this holiness, this grace which acts in your souls and in your hearts, this grace which you receive by the Sacrament of Holy Eucharist and by the Holy Mass which you offer, which you alone are capable of offering.

I shall finish, my dearly beloved brethren, by what I shall call my testament. Testament—that is a very profound word—because I want it to be the echo of the testament of Our Lord: *Novi et aeterni testamenti.*

Novi et aeterni testamenti—it is the priest who recites these words at the consecration of the Precious Blood—*Hic est enim calix Sanguinis mei: novi et aeterni testamenti.* This inheritance which Jesus Christ gave to us, it is His Sacrifice, it is His Blood, it is His Cross, the ferment of all Christian civilization and of all that is necessary for salvation.

And I say to you as well: for the glory of the Most Blessed Trinity, for the love of Our Lord Jesus Christ, for the devotion to the Blessed Virgin Mary, for the love of the Church, for the love of the Pope, for the love of bishops, of priests, of all the faithful, for the salvation of the world, for the salvation of souls, keep this testament of Our Lord Jesus Christ! Keep the Sacrifice of Our Lord Jesus Christ. Keep the Mass of All Time!

And you will see civilization reflourish, a civilization which is not of this world, but a civilization which leads to the Catholic City which is heaven. The Catholic city of this world is made for nothing else than for the Catholic City of heaven.

Thus by keeping the Blood of Our Lord Jesus Christ, by keeping His Sacrifice, by keeping this Mass—this Mass which has been bequeathed to us by our predecessors, this Mass which has been transmitted from the time of the Apostles unto this day. In a few moments I am going to pronounce these words above the chalice of my ordination, and how could you expect me to pronounce above the chalice of my ordination any other words but those which I pronounced 50 years ago over this same chalice—it is impossible! I cannot change the words! We shall therefore continue to pronounce the words of the consecration as our predecessors have taught us, as the Pope, bishops and priests who have been our instructors, have taught us, so that Our Lord Jesus Christ reign, and so that souls be saved through the intercession of our Good Mother in heaven.

APPENDIX III

Suggested Reading

Catholic Dogma in General

Denzinger, Henry. *The Sources of Catholic Dogma.* Marion House, 1957.

Ott, Ludwig. *Fundamentals of Catholic Dogma.* TAN Books and Publishers, 1974.

Pope St. Pius X. *The Catechism of Pope St. Pius X.* Instauratio Press, 1993.

The Catechism of the Council of Trent. TAN Books and Publishers, 1982.

The Crisis in the Church

Amerio, Romano. *Iota Unum: A Study of Changes in the Catholic Church in the 20th Century.* Sarto House, 1996.

De Proença Sigaud, Bishop Gerald. *What Vatican II Should Have Done.* Angelus Press, 1996.

Gaudron, Rev. Matthias. *The Catechism of the Crisis in the Church.* Angelus Press, 2010.

Lefebvre, Archbishop Marcel. *A Bishop Speaks.* Angelus Press, 1987.

———. *Against the Heresies.* Angelus Press, 1997.

———. *Open Letter to Confused Catholics.* Angelus Press, 1986.

———. *They Have Uncrowned Him.* Angelus Press, 1988.

Archbishop Lefebvre and the Society of Saint Pius X

Anglés, Fr. Ramón. *The Validity of Confessions and Marriages in the Chapels of the Society of Saint Pius X.* The Society of Saint Pius X, 1997.

Davies, Michael. *Apologia Pro Marcel Lefebvre,* Part I. Angelus Press, 1979.

Hanu, Jose. *Vatican Encounter.* Sheed Andrews & McMeel, 1978.

Laisney, Fr. François. *Archbishop Lefebvre and the Vatican.* Angelus Press, 1988.

Nemeth, Charles P. *The Case of Archbishop Lefebvre: Trial by Canon Law.* Angelus Press, 1994.

Pivert, Fr. François. *Schism or Not? The 1988 Episcopal Consecrations of Archbishop Lefebvre.* Angelus Press, 1995.

Tissier de Mallerais, Bishop Bernard. *Supplied Jurisdiction and Traditional Priests.* Angelus Press, 1993.

———. *Marcel Lefebvre.* Angelus Press, 2005.

Various authors. *Is Tradition Excommunicated?* Angelus Press, 1993.

The Second Vatican Council

Davies, Michael. *Pope John's Council,* 2nd ed. Angelus Press, 2007.

———. *The Second Vatican Council and Religious Liberty.* Neumann Press, 1992.

Fr. Pierre-Marie. *Religious Liberty: Is "Dignitatis Humanae" Compatible with Tradition?* Pace Print, 1994.

Lefebvre, Archbishop Marcel. *I Accuse the Council.* Angelus Press, 1982.

Schillebeeckx, E. *Vatican II: The Real Achievement.* Sheed & Ward, 1967.

Schmidberger, Fr. Franz. *The Catholic Church and Vatican II.* Angelus Press, 1996.

Wiltgen, Ralph. *The Rhine Flows into the Tiber.* Hawthorn Books, 1967.

The New Order of Mass

Davies, Michael. *Pope Paul's New Mass.* Angelus Press, 1980.

———. *The Barbarians Have Taken Over.* Angelus Press, 1985.

———. *The New Mass.* Angelus Press, 1980.

Ottaviani and Bacci, Cardinals. *Short Critical Study of the New Order of Mass.* TAN Books and Publishers, 1992.

Pope John Paul II

Dörmann, Fr. Johannes. *Pope John Paul II's Theological Journey to the Prayer Meeting of Religions in Assisi.* Part I, *From the Second Vatican Council to the Papal Elections.* Angelus Press, 1994.

————. *Pope John Paul II's Theological Journey to the Prayer Meeting of Religions in Assisi.* Part II, Vol. 1, *The Trinitarian Trilogy.* Angelus Press, 1996.

Le Roux, Daniel. *Peter, Lovest Thou Me?* Instauratio Press, 1989.

A Short History of the Society of Saint Pius X

Transcription of a conference given by Rev. Fr. Ramón Anglés.

(Reprinted from *The Angelus*, January 1996)

The information from 1996 to 2011 was compiled by Angelus Press.

The history of the Society of Saint Pius X begins, of course, in the mind of God. But do not believe that its temporal origin is to be found solely at the time of the post-Conciliar crisis. The Society of Saint Pius X was made possible by the providential foresight of an extraordinary man, Father Le Floch, superior of the French Seminary in Rome, who in the 1920's formed a group of future prelates and priests who, having been warned by him of the dangers of the Modernist infiltration in the Church, remained faithfully attached to her traditions

Fr. Le Floch (first row, center), Marcel Lefebvre (second row, first on left), and seminarians at the French Seminary of Rome

in the neo-Protestant Revolution. Father Le Floch announced in 1926: "The heresy which is now being born will become the most dangerous of all; the exaggeration of the respect due to the Pope and the illegitimate extension of his infallibility."

A grateful Archbishop Lefebvre often spoke of his great teacher, and we will see how in this historical recollection appear again and again figures of ecclesiastics close to the Society of Saint Pius X who studied with our founder under the exemplary guide and example of Father Le Floch.

1968

April 11, 1968, Maundy Thursday. In the little Swiss village of Saxon, Alfonse Pedroni is in the town's cafe. He hears a pompous businessman bragging that in a few months he will be able to dynamite the chapel and old farm of Ecône. The contract is going to be signed shortly. Before the day is over, Alfonse and Marcel Pedroni and their friends Gratien Rausis, Roger Lovey and Guy Genoud decide to buy the property, once owned by the Canons of St. Bernard, and containing the shrine of Our Lady of the Fields. They visit Bishop Adam of Sion to let him know of their intentions. The Bishop congratulates them but says that the Church is in crisis of vocations and there is no hope for Ecône to be saved and used as they would like as a house of formation. During the week that follows, these Catholic gen-

Archbishop Lefebvre as the new General Superior of the Holy Ghost Fathers visits the Orphanage of Auteuil, France, which the Holy Ghost Fathers had had in their charge since 1923.

The old farm of Ecône

Archbishop Lefebvre is with
Marcel Pedroni, one of the
businessmen who helped buy Ecône.

tlemen learn that the business-man intends to build in Ecône a complex of nightclub, restaurant and motel. On May 31, Feast of the Queenship of Mary, the Canons sell Ecône, not to the disappointed developer but to Alphonse and his friends, who have obtained an emergency loan from the bank. They are happy, but they do not know ex-actly what they are going to do with the property they have saved from desecration.

Also in 1968, the General Chapter of the Fathers of the Holy Ghost revises its Constitutions in the spirit of the Council. Archbishop Marcel Lefebvre, Superior General, protests before the Sacred Congregation of Religious in Rome and he is invited to take a break and to go on vacation. He presents his resignation and re-tires as chaplain to a convent in Rome.

In May 1968, in the French Seminary of Rome, the Communist flag hangs from the main balcony in support of the revolutionary students in Paris. A minuscule group of seminarians, still dressed in their cassocks and being shunned by the rest of their comrades and teachers, turn for help to Archbishop Lefebvre. He directs them to the still-conservative University of Fribourg in Switzerland, encour-

(Top right) Archbishop Lefebvre moved his seminarians from the Don Bosco House to the St. Pius X House in Fribourg. (Above) Archbishop Lefebvre with Bishop Adam of Sion at Ecône. (Bottom right) The seminary of Ecône.

aged by the Abbot of Hauterive and the Dominican theologian, Father Philippe. The Archbishop told us about this early endeavor:

> I said to these gentlemen that wanted to force me to do some-thing for the seminarians, asking me to take care of them personally, "I'm going to see Bishop Charrière; if he tells me, 'go ahead,' then I will see in it a sign of the will of God." I said this because I really didn't want to; I felt old and I was sure that I could not undertake such a work. When you are 65 years old you do not undertake a work like the one of the Society. Had somebody told me the number of priests and what the Society would be today I would just have smiled sweetly. So I didn't want to, but Bishop Charrière insisted, "*Il faut, il faut,* you must, you must; *faites, faites,* do it, do it! Do something, rent a house, don't abandon these seminarians. You know what's going on in the Church. We need absolutely to keep the good traditions." This was the sign. The Society is therefore not a personal work; it would never have been blessed by God as it has been. It was definitely a work of God.

1970

And then, as a supplementary proof that the Bishop of Lausanne, Geneva, and Fribourg wanted us to exist, on the 1st of November, 1970, he approves and confirms the constitutions and proceeds to the canonical foundation of the International Priestly Society of Saint Pius X in his diocese. (See *The Angelus*, November 1995.)

Meanwhile, the Swiss laymen offer the property of Ecône to Archbishop Lefebvre via a local parish priest, Father Bonvin, confrere of the Archbishop in the French Seminary at Rome. The seminarians leave the rented twelve rooms of the Don Bosco House in Fribourg and in September 1970, the first year starts at Ecône with the warm approval of Bishop Adam of Sion.

1971-1976

The Archbishop expected to wait a long time before the second canonical step, the approval of Rome, was effected. Only four months elapse until February 18, 1971, when Cardinal Wright, prefect for the Sacred Congregation for the Clergy, officially approves and encourages the Society. The Roman document recognizes the Society's international character and the fact that many bishops from the world praise and approve it. The Cardinal

Cardinal Wright, Prefect for the Sacred Congregation for the Clergy

is happy that the Society will contribute to the distribution of the Catholic clergy in the world.

Much to the surprise of our founder, his small work of faith receives a further encouragement. When a few priests from the outside wish to join him in the Society's work, the Archbishop submits the case to Rome, and the Roman Curia, anticipating his desires,

**Archbishop Annibal Bugnini,
architect of the *Novus Ordo Missae***

detaches totally these priests from their bishops and even from their religious orders to make them depend exclusively on the Society of Saint Pius X. This official act of Rome recognizes the right of the Society of Saint Pius X to incardinate its members.

In the vicissitudes of the years to come the Modernist Rome will publicly disapprove our Society, its fruits, and its spirit. It matters little when we know that the Rome faithful to tradition approved the Society and sent it in official mission to maintain the Catholic priesthood. Ultimately, this mandate of the Church constitutes the main reason and necessity for the episcopal consecrations of 1988.

On April 3, 1969, the Apostolic Constitution *Missale Romanum* presented a new order of the Mass. Archbishop Lefebvre gathered together a group of twelve theologians who wrote under his direction the Brief Critical Examination of the *Novus Ordo Missae* often called the Ottaviani Intervention. Cardinals Ottaviani and Bacci wrote indeed an introduction and presented the study to Paul VI. Since no response came from the Vatican, the Archbishop announces to his small group of seminarians, June 10, 1971, that he refuses to accept this new protestantized liturgy: "How can I agree to abandon the Mass of all ages or to admit to place it at the same level as the *Novus Ordo*, created by Annibale Bugnini, with the participation of Protestants, to make of it an equivocal supper that eliminates totally the Offertory and touches the very words of the Consecration."

In 1971, twenty-four candidates enter the seminary of Ecône. Thirty-two more will join them in October, 1972. But during the Christmas vacation, trouble starts. The French bishops, eager accomplices of the Modernist conspirators, are watching closely every step of the expansion of the young Society. Cardinal Lefebvre, his cousin, had already warned the Archbishop "the French episcopate will never forgive you for what you did in the Council." Jealous and worried by the unexpected success, they start a campaign of discredit. The Archbishop knew about those jealousies and he had already proposed Cardinal Marty to meet the bishops at the coming Episcopal Conference at Lourdes to explain to them the situation of Ecône. The Cardinal insisted that there was going to be no question of Ecône at this meeting. But the Episcopal Conference in Lourdes labels Ecône as "the wildcat seminary," as if they didn't know that its canonical situation was perfectly regular and that the seminary did not depend on their jurisdiction.

In 1973 an ephemeral pre-seminary is opened in Fribourg, but only for a few months, to be closed because of the worsening conditions in the University.

Society seminaries are opened at Armada, Michigan (1973), and Albano, Rome (1974). The plot to close Ecône continues and the French bishops put pressure on Rome to suppress the Society. They are afraid that traditional priests will return into their dioceses creating a traditional Catholic resistance. It is probably at this point that Cardinal Villot persuades Paul VI to believe that our seminarians must take an oath against the Pope. Villot will say to Cardinal Etchegaray, who repeated it widely, "In six months Ecône will not exist."

November 11, 1974: After breakfast, the Archbishop assembles the community to announce the arrival the same day of two apostolic visitors from Rome. They speak to the seminarians and professors, maintaining scandalous opinions such as: the ordination of married

Ecône, Class of 1971

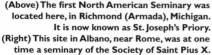

(Above) The first North American Seminary was located here, in Richmond (Armada), Michigan. It is now known as St. Joseph's Priory. (Right) This site in Albano, near Rome, was at one time a seminary of the Society of Saint Pius X.

men will soon be a normal thing, truth changes with the times, and the traditional conception of the Resurrection of our Lord is open to discussion. These remarks prompt Archbishop Lefebvre to write his famous Declaration of November 21. While Paul VI speaks openly about the auto-demolition of the Church, Archbishop Lefebvre proclaims his adhesion to the eternal Rome and his refusal of the neo-Modernist and neo-Protestant Rome of Vatican II:

> To insure our salvation the only attitude of fidelity to the Church and to Catholic doctrine is a categorical refusal to accept the Reformation. We will pursue our work of the formation of priests under the star of the age-old magisterium in the conviction that we can thus do no greater service to the Church, to the Pope, and to future generations.

Nineteen seventy-five starts with a large-scale press campaign against the Archbishop. Vandalism thickens the atmosphere around the seminary; graffiti, nocturnal phone calls, shooting of the windows, night trespassing. On February 13, three cardinals interrogate Archbishop Lefebvre, and one of them, French Cardinal Garrone, calls him "a fool." Against the provisions of Canon Law, the Society is invalidly suppressed May 6, 1975. French Cardinal Villot forces Cardinal Staffa to refuse the Archbishop's rightful canonical appeal to the Supreme Apostolic Signatura, the higher instance tribunal in the Church. The Secretary of State writes all the bishops of the world, asking them to refuse incardination to the members of the Society. The trap is now set: Without incardination there will be no priestly work, and since the Society is supposedly suppressed Archbishop Lefebvre can no longer ordain priests for our institute. He answers this illegal condemnation with a pilgrimage to Rome of the whole Society to gain the indulgences of the Holy Year, 1975.

Paul VI, in the consistory of May, 1976, denounces the Archbishop as "disobedient to the new liturgy." Cardinal Benelli asks the Archbishop to celebrate the New Mass at least once, promising in the name of the Pope that this gesture will suffice to solve the difficulties. The Archbishop refuses and, June 29, he ordains publicly in the field of Ecône twelve priests for the Society. The 23rd of July, a *suspensio a divinis* forbids him to celebrate the New Mass, as the Archbishop says with humor, and also to ordain priests because the Society doesn't exist any more.

The weeks that follow the condemnation are the opportunity for thousands of faithful to manifest publicly their attachment to Archbishop Lefebvre. More than 10,000 assemble in Lille, in the middle of summer, to show their support.

Led by Archbishop Lefebvre, the Credo Pilgrimage to Rome (May 1975) processes through St. Peter's Square.

The Mass at Lille. Archbishop Lefebvre is confronted by the media.

Instead of the excommunication joyfully announced by the media, on September 11, Pope Paul VI receives the Archbishop privately at Castel Gandolfo. During this meeting it becomes obvious that the Pope is being deliberately misinformed by dishonest collaborators.

1977

In February, 1977 traditional Catholics liberate the church of St. Nicolas du Chardonnet in Paris. Msgr. François Ducaud- Bourget and Father Coache summon the faithful for a conference in support of the Archbishop, and direct them to the old church of St. Nicolas, only a few yards away. An astonished parish priest who is celebrating the New Mass for about forty people has just announced that the church would be open only two days a week. Suddenly he sees an immense crowd filling the church respectfully and in reverent silence. A miracle? Yes, indeed, since at the end of this Mass, a processional cross announces the arrival from the street of the clergy who are going to celebrate the True Mass on the true altar. The supper table is removed, the priest escorted to the door, and the miracle of St. Nicolas continues until today.

Fall 1977 sees thirty-eight new seminarians, despite the condemnations. In October, the Society has 40 priests, 150 seminarians, 20 priories, and 3 seminaries. The Sisters of the Society, founded in 1974, move their novitiate to Albano, and their general house to St. Michel-en-Brenne under the direction of Mother Mary Gabriel Lefebvre.

1978

Nineteen seventy-eight sees the acquisition of four priories in France, a property in Long Island, and the priory of Madrid. The German seminary of Weissbad moves to Zaitzkofen. The Jesuit College of St. Mary's, Kansas, is also bought by the Society.

On November 16, the new Pope John Paul II receives the Archbishop in Rome. After a long conversation the Pope is will-

On Sunday, February 27, 1977, at Paris, the pastor of St. Nicolas du Chardonnet was just finishing up his Mass. The service was taking place on a little table set on a platform; the Mass was said in the vernacular, with the priest facing the people, of course, and his back to the altar and the east, which has always symbolized Christ. Thus turned, he saw a strange sight. The nearly empty church filled. The *Credo* was intoned, and then a procession of choir boys advanced, preceding priests vested in alb and chasuble....The Mass of St. Pius V was going to be celebrated. This was the beginning of the takeover of the church, a successful operation, at the head of which was Msgr. Ducaud Bourget. The "occupation" took place, celebrated from the pulpit by the poetic speech of the courageous chaplain of the Order of Malta, Msgr. Ducaud Bourget.

ing enough to remove all restrictions on the traditional Mass, but Cardinal Seper standing back exclaims immediately, "They make a banner of this Mass," a remark which makes a negative impression on the Pope.

Meanwhile in Argentina, a humble seminary opens in Venezuela Street, in Buenos Aires, with twelve candidates.

1979

In June, an old inn is purchased at Rickenbach (Switzerland) to be our first General House. During summer, a large property is bought twenty kilometers north of Turin at Montalenghe (Italy), for a retreat house. The American Seminary transfers to Ridgefield, Connecticut.

August 15, the Archbishop is in St. Marys, Kansas, for the first Marian Pilgrimage:

> It was a magnificent success. More than two thousand people came from everywhere. I wish that this place become a great sanctuary for all America, and a center of devotion and prayers towards the Blessed Virgin, who alone is capable of stopping the moral corruption which does not cease to grow in this immense country.

Archbishop Lefebvre celebrates his golden jubilee in Paris.

And about France:

The experience of our first two schools of St. Michel in Chateauroux and of l'Etoile du Matin gives us great hopes for the truly Christian formation of young men and for vocations that will certainly spring in such an excellent atmosphere. May God allow our schools to multiply.

The year is crowned on September 23 by the celebration of the priestly golden jubilee of the Archbishop in Paris, where he calls for a Catholic Crusade of restoration:

We must make a Crusade founded on the sacrifice of the Mass, to re-create Christendom as the Church wants it, on the same principles, the same Mass, the same sacraments, the same catechism, the same Holy Scripture. A crusade of young people, of Catholic families, of heads of families, a crusade of priests. (Archbishop Marcel Lefebvre, *Collected Works*, Vol. 1 [Angelus Press])

1980

On the occasion of our tenth anniversary, the Archbishop writes:

Our attitude for the last ten years must continue now without hesitation for the good of the Church, to help the authorities of the Church who want it to come out from the disorder in which they

have imprudently engaged themselves. The conclusion of this anniversary must be *depositum cus-
todire,* to keep the deposit of the
faith, source of grace and sanctification.

In France, the Archbishop announces the opening of "Facultés
Catholiques St. Pie X," named soon
afterwards "Institut Universitaire
St. Pie X." He writes: "The teachers
themselves have urged this foundation by addressing the Society of
Saint Pius X as the only institution
capable of maintaining a sure and
permanent doctrine for those spir-
its thirsty of truth."

In May, he visits the United
States. May 23: "*C'est magnifique,
c'est une cathédrale.*" The delicately
nasal French voice of Archbishop
Lefebvre echoes within the walls
of St. Vincent de Paul's Church
in Kansas City. Built in 1922, for

(Above) St. Vincent de Paul, Kansas City, Missouri,
as it appears now with 600 members and 115
children in the parish school. (Below) Archbishop
Lefebvre's initial plan was to make of St. Mary's
in Kansas the North American Seminary of the
Society of Saint Pius X. As Providence would have
it, the former Jesuit retreat house in Ridgefield,
Connecticut, would become its eventual location.

more than one half century the church was under the care of the
Vincentian Fathers. After the Council, eleven churches closed in the
metropolitan area, and St. Vincent's was sold to a non-denomina-
tional group; then it reverted to the diocese, which held it in trust
until its sale to the Crusaders Community Church. The rest is history. The classic beauty of this building is a standing testimony to
the love of the Church by American Catholics in an era of faith:

> I have been able to confirm with great satisfaction the extraor-
> dinary development of the groups of faithful Catholics both at the
> chapels of our priest-friends and in the Society. St. Mary's College,
> the school of St. Louis, Missouri, the beautiful chapel and rectory of

Phoenix, and, at the last moment, the acquisition of a big church in Kansas City are reasons to hope for the continuation of the Church in the United States.

Ecône sees the arrival of nine seminarians from Argentina who have come to finish their theology, but first need to learn French and Latin.

In Ridgefield we have twelve new candidates. Archbishop Lefebvre says: "We are asked from everywhere in the world to form and send priests. As of today I would need to have 150 or 200 extra priests to answer the requests of the faithful."

1981

During an early year visit to the States, Archbishop Lefebvre dedicates the complex of Jesus and Mary in El Paso, Texas. In the afternoon of January 4, 200 children are confirmed. On January 6, four years after a visa had been denied to Archbishop Lefebvre due to pressure put on the government by the bishops of Mexico, our founder crosses the border for what turns out to be a triumphant tour of the country of the Cristeros (see *The Angelus*, Dec. 1993). Followed continuously by the Mexican secret police, the Archbishop visits in the south of the country large areas of very poor Indians who, astonished, received an affirmative answer to their request for a truly Catholic bishop coming to support their fight for the Faith before the Communist clergy, sold to Liberation Theology. He is received like a conquering hero, walking among cheering crowds of thousands of villages festooned with ribbons, garlands, and the magnificent fragrant flowers of those latitudes. Some natives walk as much as

In January of 1981, hundreds of Mexican Catholics are thrilled to greet *"el hombre justo"* ("the just man"), Archbishop Marcel Lefebvre.

a hundred miles through mountains to bring their children to be confirmed and to be able to kiss the episcopal ring and receive the blessing of Marcel Lefebvre, *"el hombre justo."* In Tlaxiaco, while the diocesan bishop celebrates the New Mass for twenty-five people, thousands attend the solemn ceremonies presided by Archbishop Lefebvre.

In Rome, Cardinal Seper, the Pope's delegate for the dialogue with the Society, writes on February 19, making allusion to the possibility of sending a cardinal to find a solution to the liturgical problem and the canonical situation of the Society.

The Archbishop goes for a long missionary trip to South Africa and then to Argentina, where on August 15, he lays the first stone of the seminary in La Reja, very close to Buenos Aires. He also visits Brazil at the request of Bishop Antonio de Castro Mayer who is soon going to be forced to retire from his diocese: "We hope that he will now be able to take some action at the level of the universal Church in the present crisis."

The same year he travels to Australia to prepare the foundation of the first priory in Sydney:

> I must acknowledge that the Australian priests, faithful to tradition, and the laity have worked very well during these last years. In my last trip in 1973 the groups of Sydney and Melbourne were composed by a few families; this time 700 faithful were present at the confirmations and Mass of Sydney, and almost as many in Melbourne, and about 150 in Adelaide, Perth, and also Wanganui in New Zealand. This region gives now great hope and deserves its first priory.

Seventy-five new candidates enter our seminaries.

In Rome, Cardinal Seper goes to his reward. His last letter of October does not present any solution. Traditional Catholics are the only victims of tolerance and religious freedom, when in reality they are the ones who defend the truth.

Two years after laying its cornerstone, Archbishop Lefebvre returns to perform the ordinations at Maria Corredentora Seminary in La Reja, Argentina.

1982

On March 1, St. Joseph buys for us our first church in London, seating 300 faithful.

Cardinal Joseph Ratzinger replaces Cardinal Seper as personal representative of the Pope. The Archbishop has a long interview with him in March. Rome wants us to say that even though we may have some reservations about it, the liturgical reform is good and that we just think it is less good than the old liturgy. The Archbishop says:

District Superior of Great Britain, Fr. Edward Black, celebrates Mass in the church of St. Joseph in London, England.

Now we believe that the reform is evil, poisoned by ecumenism, and we refuse to accept it and we are obliged to advise all the faithful against it. God only knows how long the reformers will close their eyes to the destruction of the faith, of the morals, of institutions.

March 20: An all-night prayer vigil is held in Martigny, near Ecône, inspired by the message of Our Lady of Fatima asking for prayer and penance. Three thousand pilgrims assist at the consecration of the world, and especially of Russia, to the Immaculate Heart of Mary. In anticipation of the present frenzy about the new millennium, Archbishop Lefebvre declares calmly and firmly: "The twenty-first century will be Catholic or it will not be at all."

At Easter time, five monsignori and twenty diocesan priests of the diocese of Campos in Brazil publish a profession of Catholic faith in the face of the present errors, a splendid document defending the pristine doctrine and traditions of the Church, writing:

> We have the absolute certainty that our position is legitimate, not by virtue of our arguments and ideas, but because we take our stand on that which the Church herself has taught us. For the Church, we wish to give our lives if it is necessary.

The first general chapter of the Society of Saint Pius X takes place in Ecône in September. In the Acts we read a declaration of principles and directives of the Society of Saint Pius X, decisions on pastoral action in the present crisis, and warnings against liturgical changes and false ecumenism, and the rejection of liberalism but also sedevacantism:

> The Society of Saint Pius X is founded on the history of the Church and upon the doctrine of theologians. It believes that the

His Excellency Bishop Antonio de Castro Mayer (seated) and these priests of the diocese of Campos, Brazil, have a story to tell in *The Mouth of the Lion.*

Fr. Franz Schmidberger with Archbishop Lefebvre.

Pope can favor the ruin of the Church by choosing and letting act bad advisors, also by signing documents and decrees which do not engage his infallibility and that cause considerable damage to the Church. Nothing is more dangerous for the Church than liberal popes who are in a continual incoherence. We pray for the Pope, but we refuse to follow him in his errors on religious freedom, ecumenism, socialism and the application of reforms destructive for the Church. Our apparent disobedience is true obedience to the Church and to the Pope as successor of Peter in the measure that he continues to maintain holy Tradition....All the members of the Society have one desire, to be submitted in filial obedience to a Rome returned to Tradition.

Fr. Franz Schmidberger is elected Vicar General with right of immediate succession as Superior General.

In the seminaries, the course of studies is extended from five to six years. We have sixty new entries in Ecône, Ridgefield, Zaitzkofen, and Buenos Aires.

1983

This is the year of the publication of the new Code of Canon Law, which expresses in canonical terms the new Conciliar conception of the Church.

Wednesday, March 1: Father Barrielle, an apostle of the Exercises of St. Ignatius, dies at Ecône, standing up like the soldier that he always was. Before his birth, his mother had consecrated him to the Blessed Virgin, asking for a boy who one day would be a priest. And priest he became, the parish priest of a large church of Marseilles. With the permission of his bishop he followed Father Vallet to preach with him the five-day Ignatian Retreats as we know them today. In 1944, he became Superior General of the Co-operators of Christ the King, a priestly institute dedicated to Ignatian retreats. In 1973, the general chapter of his congregation changed the original constitutions, and Father Barrielle wrote an official letter stating that he had never been a member of this new congregation and that he did not want to leave the one in which he had made his religious vows. As he used to say, he "remained the only member of the congregation founded by Father Vallet." He became spiritual director of the

seminary of Ecône, where he helped generations of priests, inspiring them with his zeal and giving them the key to the Exercises. This priest "with a heart of fire," as the Archbishop said of him, signed his testament: Ludovic Marie Barrielle, slave of Mary and Joseph.

The Herz Jesu Seminary in Zaitzkofen, Germany

On April 5, the Archbishop writes very openly to the Pope:

The use of this ecumenical Mass fosters a mentality which is Protestant and indifferentist, placing all religions at the same level in the manner of the Declaration of Religious Liberty, with the doctrinal foundation of the rights of man, a misunderstood concept of human dignity that has been condemned by the Society of Saint Pius X. The consequences of this spirit are deplorable and ruin the spiritual vitality of the Church. In conscience we must discourage the priests and the faithful from the use of this *Novus Ordo* if we wish that the integral Catholic faith remain alive.

Fr. Barrielle stands at Archbishop Lefebvre's left with professors of the seminary of Ecône. Third from left is Fr. Tissier de Mallerais. Second from right is Fr. Richard Williamson.

Those who maintain that the Archbishop spoke against religious freedom only in his last years should read what he wrote in 1983:

It is obvious that tradition is not compatible with the Declaration on Religious Liberty of the Council. We request a reform of the affirmations of the Council that are contrary to the official magisterium of the Church, especially the Declaration on Religious Liberty. It is impossible for me to sign anything that may hinder the Catholic faith of my infancy, as it is the case with false ecumenism, false religious freedom. I want to live and to die in the Catholic faith.

During the spring some priests in the United States leave us, pretending that the liturgy used by the Society is bad. In this they join the choir of our modernist persecutors in Rome who also say that our liturgy is not authorized. This absurd attitude unfortunately sows confusion within the faithful and seminarians in the States. This situation puts to proof the Germanic endurance of the new Superior General, Father Schmidberger. In June, twenty-eight new priests are ordained in Ecône. Ireland receives the first priest of the

Archbishop Lefebvre with Fr. Gregory Post (left) during the Archbishop's visit to the United States.

Archbishop Lefebvre and Bishop de Castro Mayer in Rio de Janeiro. Together they prepare an open letter to the Pope.

Society. The Archbishop wishes that God will bring many vocations from this island that in the past gave so many priests and missionaries to the Church.

Cardinal Ratzinger writes from Rome in July: "The Pope acknowledges the devotion of Archbishop Lefebvre and his fundamental attachment to the Holy See, expressed for instance by the exclusion of members who do not recognize the authority of the Pope."

On August 27-28, Switzerland sees the first traditional pilgrimage to Flueli, Sanctuary of St. Nicholas of Flue, with more than 4,000 faithful attending. In Ecône, sixty-five priests follow the priestly retreat, and in Ridgefield, eleven new students join the seminary after the split. In Germany, Don Bosco's School starts with fifteen students.

The priests of Campos publish a declaration about the priestly ministry in the present extraordinary period of grave crisis, explaining the canonical doctrine that allows traditional priests to hear confessions and bless marriages.

In November, the Archbishop visits the United States, confirming 360 in Ciudad Juarez in the morning, and in the afternoon 350 in El Paso. On November 5 the Archbishop blesses St. Michael's Chapel in Long Island.

On the 21st, he meets with Bishop de Castro Mayer in Rio de Janeiro. Together they prepare an open letter to the Pope:

> In our capacity as bishops of the Holy Catholic Church, successors of the Apostles, our hearts are overwhelmed at the sights throughout the world....It seems to us to remain silent in these circumstances would be to become accomplices to these wicked works (*cf.* II Jn. 11). That is why we find ourselves obliged to intervene in public before Your Holiness (considering all the measures we have undertaken in private during the last fifteen years have remained ineffectual) in order to denounce the principal causes of this dramatic situation, and to beseech Your Holiness to use his power as Successor of Peter to "confirm your brothers in the Faith (Lk. 22:32), which has been faithfully handed down to us by Apostolic Tradition. (See *The Angelus,* Jan. 1984)

The two faithful bishops present a list outlining the principal errors of the time, including an ecumenical notion of the Church, a democratic orientation, a false notion of the natural rights of man, and a Protestant notion of the Mass and of the sacraments.

1984

The Society of Saint Pius X has reached the number of 120 priests, and Ecône also counts 120 seminarians. Father Schmidberger insists on a stabilization and consolidation with a happy expansion, and to hold on to the motto, "Neither heretics nor schismatic."

The Pope, to the great scandal of Catholics traditional or not, preaches in the Lutheran temple of Rome in March. On the 10th of May, he bows before a bonze [a pagan priest] in a Buddhist temple in Thailand; at the same time the Vatican abrogates the concordat with Italy. At this point the Archbishop starts to consider seriously the necessity of an episcopal consecration.

Also in May, Mother Mary Jude is named Superior General of the Society of Saint Pius X Sisters, and in the United States the northeast and southwest districts are reunified.

Msgr. Ducaud-Bourget dies in Paris in the middle of June. Chaplain of the Order of Malta, renowned poet and writer, faithful to the traditional Mass, he was responsible for the liberation of St. Nicolas du Chardonnet. When the *Osservatore Romano* announced his suspension, in the literary pages of the same issue an article praised the latest book of a great Catholic French writer, François Ducaud-Bourget. No greater tribute could please more the ironic character of our dear Abbé.

During summer the happy expansion starts with foundations in Mexico, Colombia, South Africa, Holland, and Portugal. Our seminarians spend one month in Rome inaugurating what will become a yearly summer tradition. Directed by a priest, they are exposed during four weeks to the history, the art, and majestic beauty of the eternal city.

October 3, the Indult. The Sacred Congregation for Divine Worship communicates to the presidents of the episcopal conferences that the diocesan bishops may allow the celebration of the Mass according to the 1962 typical edition of the Roman Missal. Among the draconian conditions, public evidence should exist that the petitioners have no ties with those who deny the doctrinal soundness of the missal promulgated by Paul VI, and that the celebration may take place only on those days and circumstances approved by the bishop. The letter is

Archbishop Lefebvre appears with Sisters of the Society of Saint Pius X at their motherhouse shortly after the election of Mother Mary-Jude (from the U.S.) as Superior General of the order.

signed by Archbishop Mayer, afterwards Cardinal in charge of the Ecclesia Dei Commission. He indicates that this Indult is to be used without prejudice to the liturgical reform.

On October 18, in the so-called Document of Flavigny, the Society of Saint Pius X and forty priests and laymen leaders of traditional works refuse the conditions of the Indult and ask for a wider application without compromise regarding the Liturgical Reformation.

In November, a Gallup poll requested by traditional Catholics of Vienna, Virginia, reveals that 40 percent of American Catholics want the return to traditional Mass and that 53 percent will be happy to attend if it is restored.

Si Si No No

THE ANGELUS ENGLISH-LANGUAGE ARTICLE REPRINT

Let your speech be, "Yes, yes," "No, no", whatever is beyond these comes from the evil one. (Mt. 5:37) • **February 1995**

They Think They've Won!

HOW THEY THINK THEY'VE WON IN CATHOLIC EXEGESIS

Don Francesco Putti, founding editor of the journal *SISINONO*, Italian bi-weekly for priests now translated into many languages including the English version published by Angelus Press in its magazine, *The Angelus*

The Archbishop travels to Chile in November. Four hundred confirmations are announced in Santiago; twelve hundred arrive. During a ceremony of four hours the Archbishop proceeds to the longest confirmation session in his life.

On the 8th of December in Ecône, all the superiors make the Consecration of the Society of Saint Pius X to the Immaculate and Sorrowful Heart of Mary, prepared by an evening of prayers at Martigny attended by more than 4,000 faithful.

On December 21, Don Francesco Putti dies. A close spiritual dirigé of Padre Pio, he was a late vocation. Staunch defender of tradition in Rome, he founded the Disciples of the Cenacle, a feminine congregation, and the journal *Sì Sì No No*, which can be found hidden under every desk in the Roman Curia. Don Putti was feared by the Modernist hierarchy because of his no-nonsense approach and his tenacity that took him to sue *L'Osservatore Romano*, obtaining the first public apology that the newspaper ever published. He was with us till the end.

At the end of the year, Archbishop Lefebvre visits Cardinal Ratzinger, then goes to Africa, and at his return to Rome he sees Cardinal Gagnon, who gives shocking details of the network of conspiracy and corruption in Rome. The Archbishop comments: "The situation is even worse than what we had thought until now."

1985

Archbishop Lefebvre on television. Archbishop Lefebvre honored by a head of state and received by bishops. We are not talking about the good old days, but of the visit that in January the Archbishop paid to his missionary origins in Gabon. He had been warmly received in Senegal by Cardinal Thiandoum, and now he is officially welcomed at Libreville by President Bongo, who recalls the "excellent work accomplished by Father Lefebvre in Gabon," a well-deserved tribute that is featured in a television broadcast for all the country. The president puts his car and his private plane at the disposal of his guest and in a jubilant tour the Archbishop visits the communities and friends where his memory has remained imperishable.

Father Schmidberger writes in February:

> The best service we can give to the Church, the Pope and the Bishops, is to insist inflexibly on our position, to preach the Gospel at any cost, to continue in the way in which we are engaged, and first of all to form true priests. Our disharmony with the present Rome does not come from us but from those who have broken with tradition. It is not we who are the defendant; we are the prosecution, and this not by a caprice, nor pharisaism, but in virtue of a sacred duty and with our heart full of sorrow.

In March, Father presents to Cardinal Ratzinger three big packages with the petitions of 129,849 traditional Catholics asking the Pope to solve the problem of tradition.

Meanwhile, the Archbishop writes his *Open Letter to Confused Catholics*.

At Chartres, France, 8,000 faithful attend the pilgrimage of tradition. At the end a message of encouragement from Cardinal Gagnon is read.

Mexico: during the Holy Week in Tlaxiaco, 15,000 faithful Indians attend the Palm Sunday procession and 2,500 confessions are heard during the holy days.

At the end of July, the Society of Saint Pius X preaches retreats in Lebanon. During summer: Missionary trips to India, Ceylon and Gabon, where two bishops encourage a foundation. Cardinal Thiandoum says: "The Society of Saint Pius X could form in the whole world a clergy rooted in the faith; Ecône would turn into an example for the formation of priests in our times."

In Ireland, a new church is bought in Dublin seating 700 faithful, and ten new chapels open in Germany. A world-wide campaign led by

Thousands of pilgrims prepare to depart Montmartre at the foot of the Basilica of the Sacred Heart in Paris for the Cathedral of Notre Dame in Chartres, France, 60 miles away.

(Above) Lady Kinnoull
(Left) St. John's Church,
Dublin, Ireland

the Society of Saint Pius X protests against the blasphemous film *Hail Mary*.

On July 22, Lady Kinnoull dies in Carmel, California. She was the very first providential benefactress of the Society. English countess, very cultivated, knowing profoundly her religion with a solid attachment to tradition, with the character of a crusader, and with a great fortune, she supported financially General Franco during the Spanish War. Restless fighter, in 1964 she flew to Paris to meet Archbishop Lefebvre while he was still Superior General of the Holy Ghost Fathers, to tell him that her fortune and influences would be at his service if he needed help to fight against the subversion within the Church. During the first years of the Society of Saint Pius X in Fribourg she covered most of the expenses of that early foundation. At her death, the Archbishop wrote: "She could consider the young priests of the Society as her children because without her help at the beginning it would not have been possible to fulfill our priestly work."

On August 31, Archbishop Lefebvre and Bishop de Castro Mayer write another open letter to the Pope, a solemn injunction this time:

> Holy Father, your responsibility is heavily engaged in this new and false conception of the Church which is drawing clergy and faithful into heresy and schism. If the Synod of Bishops perseveres in this

direction you will no longer be the Good Shepherd. Please put an end to the invasion of Modernism within the Church.

Mother Marie Christiane, blood sister of Archbishop Lefebvre, visits the United States in October to found the American Carmel in Phoenixville, Pennsylvania.

The month of October witnesses three important declarations of the Archbishop. During a press release concerning the Extraordinary Synod of Bishops in Rome, to be held on the twentieth anniversary of the closing of the Council, he asks:

> While at the Council there was a battle between conservative Catholics and ecumenist Liberals, now we are witnessing a struggle between the Liberals themselves. Thus we have the tragedy which is to unfold. Will the Revolution carry the day yet a second time, or will it be crushed? Alas, unless God intervenes, there is every reason to believe that the Revolution will continue its devastating course.

At the end of the month, he talks about the three wars of his life: the first World War (1914-18), where he saw the destruction of whatever remained of Christian Europe; the second World War (1939-45), with the official recognition by all nations of Communism; and the third War (1962-65), the worst one, wounding the very heart of the Church, the Second Vatican Council. After it, the liberal virus is instilled openly in the hierarchy and the faithful.

In our church of Geneva, October 27, Archbishop Lefebvre asks traditional Catholics to consider our chapels as our parishes:

> We are going to find ourselves in an ecclesiastical situation more and more grave, and this is why in my opinion we are obliged more and more to separate ourselves from this Conciliar stream, if not heretical, at least openly favoring heresy. In consequence, henceforth, we must consider our places

In 1978, Mother Marie Christiane appeared with these two Carmelite novices. "Carmelites are the supernatural support for the fruitful apostolate of priests."

The Extraordinary Synod of Bishops meets in Rome (1986), held on the 20th anniversary of the closing of Vatican Council II. It prompted a strong retort from Archbishop Lefebvre.

of worship as true parishes and receive the sacraments in them, including the sacrament of marriage.

On November 6, the Archbishop places before Cardinal Ratzinger our *Dubia* on religious freedom. We will wait one year for an answer.

In La Reja, Argentina, he celebrates his eightieth birthday, November 29. On December 1, Bishop de Castro Mayer, who came from Brazil for the ordinations by Archbishop Lefebvre, and participates in the rite by imposing his hands with the other priests present on the eight new ordinands. On the 3rd of December he himself proceeds to confer the tonsure and the minor orders to our seminarians, an unexpected event that makes our Archbishop quip: "This is the first time in the history of the Society that I have attended a ceremony of ordination!"

1986

The Pope visits Togo and India, again scandalizing the faithful by taking public part in ceremonies of a pagan nature.

In January, Cardinal Gagnon calls Archbishop Lefebvre to Rome and announces that the Holy Father wants him to be associated to Cardinal Ratzinger in the Society's case.

Our house of Gabon is founded on January 14, the mission being consecrated to St. Joseph. The President invites Archbishop Lefebvre to visit the country, which he does in February, this time to leave his priests in residence.

Regular missionary trips begin to New Guinea, Japan, South Korea, and Hong Kong. The pilgrimage of Chartres brings 15,000 faithful and more than 100 priests; more than 3,000 will also attend the pilgrimage to St. Nicholas of Flue.

During the ordinations of June at Ecône, 125 priests impose hands on the young men who have come to reinforce the ranks. The priory of Wanganui, New Zealand, opens on August 16. A priory is also founded in Port du France, Martinique. Monthly Masses start in Luxembourg, and in Santiago, Chile, a big church is bought with 500 faithful in attendance. The Castle of Jaidhof is purchased in Austria to become a center of retreats and missionary work. A summer retreat in Lebanon brings sixty-five men to follow the Exercises. The Society of Saint Pius X prepares a foundation for October in Zimbabwe, and starts a timid beginning of the apostolate in India.

In the United States, at the beginning of August, the Society of Saint Pius X Sisters found a novitiate at Armada, Michigan. The headquarters of the Society moves from Dickinson, Texas, to St. Louis, Missouri.

The bishops of Gabon, who had been happy to visit with the Archbishop, but not so happy to have his priests among them, instigated by the papal nuncio, write the Archbishop expressing, of course, esteem and gratitude, but telling him also that they would like to see him reconciled with Rome. Their old superior answers on August 9, scolding them without false charity, using the words of St. Paul, to the Galatians: "I am shocked that you turn away so quickly

The Society's flourishing mission in Gabon, Africa

Sacred Heart Church in Wellington, the capital of New Zealand in southern North Island, with a population of 135,000

The Eucharistic Crusade, once numbering 3 million members under Pope Pius X, has been revived by Society priests.

The contingent of Crusaders in St. Marys, Kansas

from the one who has called you in the grace of Jesus Christ to pass to a different Gospel." And then he says:

I am in a position to repeat these words to you because I am the one who has announced to you the Gospel, the only one. The new gospel of religious freedom and of the rights of man is not the true gospel. We have a tragic choice to make, either to keep the Catholic faith and not to follow the authorities unfaithful to their task, or to follow blindly those authorities and accept a false gospel. You choose the unfaithful authorities; we choose the Gospel of our Lord, faithfully transmitted by the Church until 1960. We go to the rescue of those Catholics who have kept the sense of faith; founding a Society of Saint Pius X house in Gabon I only continue what I did from 1932 to 1945 with the approval of the Church. You are the ones who have turned away to a different gospel. The true Catholics of Gabon are fully aware of it and now they thank God because they have found the true Gospel of their infancy. The day of our judgment, God will ask us if we have been faithful, not if we have obeyed unfaithful authorities. Obedience is a virtue relative to truth and to good. When it is submitted to error and to evil it is not a virtue, but a vice. May you remain disciples of truth and not of error.

The Archbishop keeps writing in the hot summer, this time a letter addressed to conservative cardinals to warn them about the meeting of Assisi that is going to take place on October 27. He asks them to save the honor of the humiliated Church and to avoid the scandal of this meeting in which the Pope will publicly mock the first article of the Creed and the first of the Ten Commandments. "What would the Inquisition do if it still existed?" writes the Archbishop.

The new academic year sees the opening of the seminary of Flavigny in France for the spirituality and philosophy years with thirty-six seminarians.

After the scandal of the ecumenical meeting of Assisi, Bishop de Castro Mayer exercises a public episcopal ministry along with Archbishop Lefebvre, and on November 29, he confirms with great solemnity 450 children in our chapel of Buenos Aires. Meanwhile, in the Antilles, Archbishop Lefebvre is received by 250 people in Martinique and 500 in Guadaloupe.

The seminarians of Ecône restore the Eucharistic Crusade for children, now extended throughout the world.

1987

The Society has 205 priests working in 23 countries and 263 young men filling the seminaries. In Ridgefield, the arrival of nineteen new seminarians makes the house burst at the seams, and the General Council determines that it is time to move the seminary elsewhere, and to turn Ridgefield into a retreat house. St. Mary's has 700 faithful, and in France a new Carmel is founded, the seventh after the foundations started by Mother Marie Christiane Lefebvre in 1977, one Carmel for each seminary.

Curé d'Ars Seminary, Flavigny, France

January sees the death of Mother Mary Gabriel. Sister of the Holy Ghost, co-found-

The first Sisters and Mother Marie Gabriel of the newly-founded congregation of the Sisters of the Society of Saint Pius X meet with Archbishop Lefebvre in Ecône (1976). Their novitiate, first located in Albano, Rome, where the first professions took place, was fixed definitively in September 1977 at St. Michel-en-Brenne (below). Ten years later, Mother Marie Gabriel would die.

ress and first General Superior of the Sisters of the Society of Saint Pius X, missionary in Cameroon, in Banghi, in the Antilles, and Senegal, she founded the Society of the Daughters of Mary of Cameroon in Yaoundee, and devoted herself as a nurse in the leper hospital of Banghi. Always happy and humble, profoundly religious and exemplary, she was unable to accept the changes in her congregation, to the point that she felt like a stranger. With the permission of her superiors she helped her brother to found a religious congregation of women with identity of goals with the Society of Saint Pius X. A simple, happy, and strong soul, she cannot be forgotten by those who had the grace to know her.

On January 18, dies Fr. Raymond du Lac, a renowned canonist who studied at the French Seminary with Archbishop Lefebvre, remaining friends to the end. He proved canonically that the Constitution *Missale Romanum* of Paul VI did not affect the right to celebrate the traditional Mass. Until the last day he remained an energetic defender of the Roman traditions the he learned under Father Le Floch.

On March 9, Rome answers to our *Dubia*: Religious freedom, they say, constitutes a novelty that can very well be put in accord with tradition. While Rome answers in this nonchalant manner, the South American bishops announce that 60 million Catholics have joined Protestant sects, and Cardinal Ratzinger optimistically declares that "we want to assimilate in the Church the best values of two hundred years of liberal culture." Archbishop Lefebvre answers with his book, *They have Uncrowned Him.*

In Gabon, 400 faithful already attend the Society chapel regularly, which makes the Archbishop of Libreville publicly attack our work. He pressures the government, and the Fathers are notified that by the end of the school year they must close the chapel and leave the country. Only a miracle can stop the persecution and the miracle happens. On the feast of the Sacred Heart, the chief of police of Libreville comes in person to tell the astonished community that nothing is going to happen and that they may finally remain.

The Society of Saint Pius X founds in France the Confraternity for the Deliverance of the Souls in Purgatory, a work that keeps growing every year and that today is in possession of their own chapel in France.

The double scandal: (right) The Holy Father meets the Grand Rabbi Elio Toaff in the Roman Synagogue, and (left) the Assisi Prayer Meeting (1986).

In 1987 Pope John Paul II asked Canadian Edouard Cardinal Gagnon, President of the Pontifical Council for the Family, to make a month-long visit of the houses and chapels of the Society of Saint Pius X. Archbishop Lefebvre valued Card. Gagnon for his firmness in defending the patrimony of the Faith. In his letter of acceptance of this Apostolic Visitation, which he sent to Rome early in October 1987, Archbishop Lefebvre made explicitly clear that he would be pleased if Card. Gagnon were named to make the visit.

During the ordinations, the Archbishop says that after the visit of the Pope to the Synagogue of Rome and the Congress of Religions in Assisi, after all the warnings, Rome is now in the darkness. Twenty-one new priests, 130 assisting priests and 6,000 faithful are present at the historical moment when the Archbishop announces publicly that he believes it is an obligation to save the priesthood by proceeding to an episcopal consecration.

Rome, July 14. In a meeting with Cardinal Ratzinger, the Archbishop exclaims: "Your eminence, for us Jesus Christ is everything; He is the Church, He is the priesthood, He is our apostolate, He is the Catholic family, He is the Catholic state." And he adds: "If you do not name bishops to assure my succession, my duty will be to do it by myself."

After a "dialogue of deaf people" during twenty years that has become an unsuccessful monologue, everything seems to indicate that Rome is just waiting for the death of Archbishop Lefebvre to give the final stroke against traditional works.

At the end of July, Providence directs us to Winona, Minnesota, where a magnificent building that belonged to the Dominican order, after some repairs, is to receive our seminarians, presently squeezed in Ridgefield.

On July 26, Fr. Stephen Abdoo, after one year of most fruitful priestly work since his ordination, dies in a car accident in New Zealand.

July 28, Cardinal Ratzinger writes to the Archbishop offering at last concrete proposals for a solution, including the possibility of a Cardinal visiting the works of the Society.

Fatima, August 22, at the seventieth anniversary of the apparitions: 2,000 people gather for a night vigil of prayer and a Pontifical Mass during which Archbishop Lefebvre consecrates the Society of Saint Pius X to Our Lady, and inasmuch as it is in his power, he also consecrates Russia to the Immaculate Heart of Mary. During his homily he says that there is an intimate link between the secret of Fatima and the post-Conciliar crisis.

A group of cardinals and bishops ask the Pope in September to find a solution for the Society of Saint Pius X. On the 1st of October the Archbishop accepts an Apostolic Visitor to come in the name of the Pope to see what tradition is all about. The Archbishop informs the press of a certain positive change in our relations with Rome. He goes to the Eternal City to continue the negotiations and on October 29, Cardinal Ratzinger informs the Synod of Bishops that the Pope has named Cardinal Gagnon as Apostolic Visitor to the Society of Saint Pius X, much to the delight of some bishops and to the worry of others.

The great family of tradition surrounds Archbishop Lefebvre in Ecône for his forty years of episcopate on October 3. Before 80 priests, 150 seminarians, and 4,000 faithful, Archbishop Lefebvre

The Society of Saint Pius X was not the only party interested in buying this former Dominican novitiate house. Playboy Enterprises and the Betty Ford Clinic were also interested. In 1995, it houses the largest number of seminarians ever and the most of any Society seminary.

says in his homily that two mottoes have conducted his episcopal ministry, the one of the Society of Saint Pius X, "*Instaurare omnia in Christo*," and "*Credidimus Caritati*," his own episcopal motto.

In November, more involved than ever, Bishop de Castro Mayer goes to our seminary in Buenos Aires to confer the tonsure and give the

Holy Cross Seminary, near Goulburn, Australia

minor orders, as well as to ordain three subdeacons and four deacons.

The 11th of November, exactly thirteen years after the first Apostolic Visit of 1974, Cardinal Gagnon and Monsignor Perl arrive in Ecône. In a marathon visit till the 9th of December, they visit the three European seminaries, chapels, general house, groups of priests, schools, convents, retreat houses, up and down France, Germany, and Switzerland. In the Book of Honor of the seminary of Ecône, Cardinal Gagnon writes a testimony of admiration for the work done in the seminary.

On December 8, Feast of the Immaculate Conception, Cardinal Gagnon assists pontifically the Mass celebrated by Archbishop Lefebvre during which twenty-seven seminarians make their first engagement in the Society of Saint Pius X. Thus, the Holy Father's hand-picked delegate officially attends a Mass celebrated by a "suspended" bishop who receives members into a "suppressed" society which "officially" does not exist.

1988

On January 5, Cardinal Gagnon presents to the Pope a mysterious 39-page report of which no copy was ever given to us. On

February 2, the Archbishop announces in Flavigny before television cameras that he will consecrate three bishops on June 30.

Our Australian seminary, Holy Cross, opens with fourteen seminarians on the Feast of St. Joseph.

Rome is afraid. After a constant coming and going of negotiations, an obscure protocol is signed the 5th of May. The day after, the Archbishop discovers that there are no assurances that the conditions will be promptly fulfilled, and he decides to proceed to the consecrations of auxiliary bishops. It is a survival operation of Tradition, absolutely justified by the unjust persecution of faithful Catholics and the betrayal of the Faith by Roman authorities.

Ecône, June 29: at the priestly ordinations, the two faithful bishops, plus 173 priests who come from all over the world, impose hands on the ordinands. That very evening Rome makes a last attempt to avoid the consecrations, sending a beautiful black Mercedes to take the Archbishop on the spot to Rome.

On June 30, 8,000 faithful witness the historical consecration of four Catholic bishops to continue the work of Archbishop Lefebvre. This heroic action made of him, Bishop Mayer, and the four young prelates the first excommunicated of the post-Conciliar era. The reasons for which the Church rewarded him greatly until

Bishop Antonio de Castor Mayer imposes his hands on the ordinands during the ceremony of ordination held at Ecône (June 29, 1988), the day before the Episcopal Consecrations.

the death of Pius XII were now the cause of his condemnation by the New Church.

Our bishops do not have vacation, they go immediately on long confirmation trips. Bishop Williamson visits England, Ireland, South Africa, Zimbabwe, New Zealand, Australia, and Hawaii in the months following his consecration.

With the fresh chrism of consecration still on his hands, Bishop Fellay visits Asia and Australia. He finds an unexpected reception in Palayamkottai, India, where the traffic is stopped for the solemn procession in which he is driven in a triumphal carriage of stupendous form, much like the throne of an Indian maharajah, accompanied by a band and firecrackers. The locals are enchanted, the modernist bishop is not, and so he pressures the local police to forbid the confirmation ceremony. Bishop Fellay must take refuge in the house of some Protestants, and finally he is allowed to visit the chapel for a few minutes escorted by the police. So much for post-conciliar tolerance and freedom of religion.

Archbishop Lefevbre and Bishop de Castro Mayer stand with the four new bishops after the episcopal consecrations of 1988.

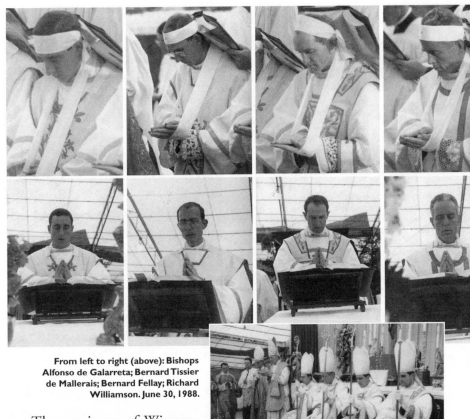

From left to right (above): Bishops Alfonso de Galarreta; Bernard Tissier de Mallerais; Bernard Fellay; Richard Williamson. June 30, 1988.

The seminary of Winona opens October 8. In Australia, our sisters open a convent in Sydney.

On October 27, Fr. Denis Marchal, one of our young priests, dies in a car accident in France. During his seminary he devoted himself to the preparation of a booklet, *The Society of Saint Pius X: A Work of the Church*. In London and in Lourdes he exercised his apostolate and he still wrote another book on the Archbishop's resistance.

November 23, death of Fr. Joseph Le Boulch, a Benedictine monk and spiritual director at Ecône. A great preacher, very well known in religious communities and parishes in France, from 1937 onwards he undertook over a thousand major preachings (retreats,

(Above) Bishop Fellay is welcomed in Palayamkottai, India, where the Society of Saint Pius X has a priory in Tuticorin from which it serves four chapels. Bishop Fellay blessed the priory (Dec. 3, 1989) on the Feast of St. Francis Xavier, "the Apostle to the Indies." Prior Rev. Fr. Eric Simonot must learn not only a difficult language but a different kind of transportation.

missions, days of recollection). He joined Archbishop Lefebvre in 1975, leaving with the permission of the superiors his dear Landevennec, an ancient abbey with a history of fifteen centuries.

Another Benedictine with a different concept of loyalty, Dom Gerard Calvet, prior of Le Barroux, breaks with the Archbishop and condemns the episcopal consecrations at which he was present, turning himself into Rome's hands "without any doctrinal or liturgical concession." In 1995, Abbot Calvet concelebrates the New Mass with John Paul II in Rome.

Rome, December 4, twenty-fifth anniversary of the liturgical reformation. An Apostolic Letter of the Pope says that the liturgical reform is absolutely traditional and according to the norms of the Holy Fathers: "*Ad normam sanctorum patrum*"!

December 8: The six Catholic bishops consecrate Russia to the Immaculate Heart of Mary.

1989

The Society of Saint Pius X starts a perpetual Mass in honor of the Immaculate and Sorrowful Heart of Mary, renewing daily its consecration to her. Perpetual Adoration is also begun and the Blessed Sacrament remains exposed at some house of the Society throughout the world every day for the faithful to pray for the following intentions: 1) the return of Rome and the bishops to the traditional doctrine of the Church; 2) the sanctification of priests and candidates for the priesthood, 3) the awakening of priestly and religious vocations.

In one year our four new bishops have ordained thirty-four new priests. The Archbishop, being asked if he has any doubt, or if he regrets the step of 1988, answers:

> Absolutely not. Everything was truly providential and almost miraculous. I was pressured from many sides for a long time and I could have ordained bishops three or four years ago; it would even have been reasonable, but I believe that God wanted things to develop slowly so that we could show to Rome and to history that we have done all we could to finally obtain the authorization to have traditional bishops. The faithful will be more and more numerous and they will open their eyes to see finally what is the truth in this affair. They will understand that salvation is in the Catholic Church and not in the Conciliar Church that becomes more and more schis-

The first ordinations from St. Thomas Aquinas Seminary, Winona, Minnesota. From left to right in front row: Rev. Frs. Paul Kimball, J. Timothy Pfeiffer, Paul Tague, and John Young.

Twenty-three thousand assist at the Mass of Archbishop Lefebvre's 60th Priestly Jubilee at Le Bourget in France.

matic. I know that my name has been removed from the *Pontifical Directory* this year, but I hope that it has not disappeared from the *Directory* of our dear Lord, and this is what matters.

Winona sees the first priestly ordinations in the new seminary. In France, summer study sessions for priests on theological subjects start and continue successfully until today.

Rome, September: the Pope writes to all Moslems of the world saying that he addresses them "in the name of the same God that we adore."

While the Pope adores Allah, on November 19, in Le Bourget, 23,000 faithful gather together to adore the Triune God and to thank Him on the occasion of the sixtieth Priestly Jubilee of the Archbishop.

Italy, December 1: Katharina Tangari dies at the seminary of Albano. Spiritual daughter of Padre Pio, she was commanded by him to consecrate her life to help the priests and the Catholic faithful in Communist countries, bringing them financial help, medicines, books and religious objects to help them to keep their faith. Madame Tangari continued this apostolate, helping the priests of the Society of Saint Pius X to the point that there is not one country in the traditional world which has not been in some way benefitted by her generosity and dedication. Purified by a long prison term in Czechoslovakia under the Communist KGB, she was not afraid of taking a public stand for Archbishop Lefebvre and his works. A truly saintly soul, she continues to help us from her well-deserved rest in heaven.

1990

No doubt that it was Madame Tangari who from heaven made possible the beginning of our Eastern European apostolate. On May 23, Father Schmidberger visits Hungary and celebrates a Mass in a Budapest church for 200 faithful.

On April 29, twenty years of the Society are celebrated before 10,000 faithful in Friedrichshafen, but the earthly crown of the Archbishop is still a crown of thorns. He is accused of racism and calumny by the LICRA (League Against Racism and Anti-Semitism). Cardinal Thiandoum, the African prelate ordained priest by the Archbishop, makes an indignant public declaration against the accusations and in favor of the great missionary Archbishop of Dakar who left in Africa an extraordinary memory. The president of Gabon defends "the good Archbishop who spent thirty years in Africa doing only good." What an irony it is to condemn as racist the only prelate who received from African governments the highest decorations as the Equatorial Star of Gabon and the Grand National Order of Senegal, as well as the Legion of Honor from France for

Archbishop Lefebvre delivers the sermon during the Mass celebrating the 20th anniversary of the Society of St. Pius X in Friedrichshafen, Germany.

Holy Family School, Lauzon, Quebec, Canada

overseas services. At this time he finishes his book, *Spiritual Journey.*

The Carmelites move to Spokane, Washington. In Ridgefield the great number of retreatants make us realize that a new retreat house is needed immediately for the Southwest.

Canada, September 10: A magnificent building in Lauzon, Quebec, houses the big school of the Holy Family starting with forty-two students.

In Gabon, 3,000 faithful attend the Christmas Mass in our mission. Also at Christmas time, our sisters' novitiate moves from Armada to Browerville, Minnesota.

1991

On March 25, Archbishop Lefebvre dies. It is the day of the priestly ordination of our Lord in the bosom of His Mother, and according to the ancient martyrologies it is also the date of the death of our Savior. On his tombstone we put the words that he wanted, "*Tradidi quod et accepi,*" "I have transmitted what I received."

Exactly one month later, on April 25, Bishop de Castro Mayer follows him to heaven.

To fulfill the wish expressed last February by the two late prelates, the bishops of the Society consecrate Msgr. Licinio Rangel, on July 28, to continue in Brazil the survival operation of the Catholic Faith. After the retiring of Bishop de Castro Mayer, his successor, Bishop Navarro, had proceeded to the systematic persecution of all the traditional priests in Campos, removing them from their parishes and forcing in the New Mass and the new religion. The Catholic re-

The crypt temporarily holding Archbishop Lefebvre's remains, soon to be transferred to the new church being built in Ecône

sistance was centered around the person of Bishop de Castro Mayer. After his death, his priests and thousands of faithful needed a bishop who, without claiming a personal jurisdiction, would use his episcopal faculties to ordain, to confirm, and to sustain the faith among the Catholic people in the present crisis.

Bishop Antonio de Castro Mayer

This year also sees the death of Dom Edouard Guillou on May 19. A monk of Solesmes, a specialist in liturgy and in art, writer in history and literature, he was one of the early teachers of Ecône in 1974. He instilled in the early seminarians the love for the Roman liturgy and for the spirit of Dom Gueranger, author of *The Liturgical Year*. A man of convictions and sempiternal good humor he used to repeat, "Never hide your flag in your pocket."

In the U.S. district, a property is bought in Los Gatos, California, in order to make possible a very much-needed new retreat center.

1992

Energetic start of missionary work in Eastern Europe: Prague, Budapest, visits to Poland, Lithuania, the Ukraine, and Russia. Itinerant missionary priests of the Society also visit Kenya, Sri Lanka, and the Dominican Republic. In order to implore the Master of the Vineyard to send laborers into the field, the Society launches a crusade for vocations.

January 14: Father Spiq, a Dominican, internationally renowned scriptural scholar, dies in Switzerland. He was also one of the early professors who helped Archbishop Lefebvre to form the first seminarians.

United States, May 13: official opening of the Regina Coeli House. Father Schmidberger blesses the new District Headquarters and consecrates the U.S. District to the Immaculate Heart of Mary.

Cardinal Oddi oddly appears in the seminary of Ecône for a sudden visit. After praying before the tomb of the Archbishop he exclaims in his unique Italian flamboyance *"Merci Monseigneur, Thank you Archbishop."* Father Schmidberger writes him shortly afterwards:

> There are three stages, Your Eminence, in the present crisis: 1) to admit that we live in a very grave crisis, and not in a new Pentecost of the Church; 2) we analyze the foundations of this crisis using the teachings of the popes in the past two centuries, as the crisis is not just a question of Latin; 3) we draw conclusions and also take concrete measures so that we do not remain at a Platonic level. Archbishop Lefebvre and Bishop Castro-Mayer arrived at the third stage on June 30, 1988.

Philippines, August 18: The first priory of the Philippines is founded in Manila.

United States, September 3: Bishop Williamson blesses the beautiful church of St. Pius X in Cincinnati, Ohio.

Brussels, September 13: Three hundred religious leaders–Christian, Buddhist, Jews, Moslems, Hindus, Animists–are invited by Cardinal Daneels to pray for the world's peace, rejecting that our Lord Jesus Christ is the only one Who can bring peace to the

Our Lady of Victories Priory in Manila

Silvio Cardinal Oddi thanked the Archbishop at his very tomb.

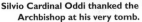

The new General House of the Society of Saint Pius X in Menzingen, Switzerland. "International Headquarters."

A victim soul, Fr. Henri La Praz performed this, his last baptism, at Our Lady of Lepanto, July 19, 1992.

world. Buddha, Krishna, Allah, *donate nobis pacem.* The Society organizes a concentration of Catholics for a ceremony of reparation for the Cardinal's sin with the public prayer of the Stations of the Cross.

Buenos Aires, October 12: The Congress of the Fifth Centenary of the Discovery of America and Its Christianization assembles illustrious speakers who emphasize the need of a re-Christianization of the large continent that Columbus and Queen Isabella offered to Christ the King.

1993

Forty-one priests gather at St. Thomas Aquinas Seminary in Winona for the third annual Priests' (U.S. District) Meeting.

In April, the General House is transferred to Menzingen, Switzerland, in the Canton of Zug.

The conservative international magazine *30 Days* publishes two interviews and an article presenting our doctrinal position.

The relations with Eastern Europe become more intense: 110 Ukrainians in three big buses visit Ecône, and 20 Russians spend one week at the seminary of Zaitzkofen. Our priests start to visit Albania, Byelorussia, and the Baltic countries.

Father Paradis, an old Canadian priest, in Shawinigan since 1985, goes to his eternal reward. On May 21 our Fr. Henri La Praz consummates his Calvary on earth. One hundred and thirty surgeries, eighty of them under general anesthesia and a good number of the last ones without any anesthesia at all, mark a life of cheerful suffering which makes of Father La Praz priest and victim as our Lord Jesus Christ, an extraordinary and unique soul.

During the summer, 400 retreatants attend the five-day Ignatian Exercises preached in South America.

Father Schmidberger, indefatigable, repeats his motto again in a letter to the Society members:

> We are not liberals nor schismatic; we are Catholic, Roman Catholic. We want to be the heirs of St. Thomas Aquinas, of Saint Pius V, of the Society of Saint Pius X. We are the children of Archbishop Lefebvre. We do not want any particular spirituality, we make ours the one of the Holy Church of our Lord Jesus Christ, priest and victim, prophet and king. The holiness of the Church is not to be found in the new liturgy, in the relativist ecumenism, nor in the naturalist laicization of the nations. The sanctity of the Church is to be found in holy tradition.

And so the work of tradition continues and our priests go to teach all nations. This year they will visit Moscow, Denmark, Sweden, Norway, and Guatemala on a regular schedule, and, at the same time that the house is bought in Fatima, just behind the Basilica of Our Lady, the General Superior opens an headquarters priory based in Austria to take care of the spiritual needs of all of

The newly elected Superior General, Bishop Bernard Fellay, pictured in the courtyard at Ecône, is flanked by his first and second assistants: Fr. Franz Schmidberger on his right and Fr. Paul Aulagnier on his left.

Eastern Europe and to co-ordinate our apostolate in this immense region.

1994

In July, the General Chapter of the Society of Saint Pius X, assembled at Ecône, proceeds to the election of a new Superior General in the person of Bishop Bernard Fellay. After a spiritual retreat, the forty participants in the chapter elect the new Superior General and his assistants, and during four days they discuss the problems and challenges of the Society apostolate worldwide. All those assisting renew the Consecration to the Immaculate Heart of Mary, and the Chapter finishes with the Enthronement of the Sacred Heart in our work.

August 6: Another encyclical comes to darken and confuse the Church—*Veritatis Splendor*, a document of liberal tenor presenting a naturalist interpretation of the mysteries of Incarnation and Redemption, with an anthropocentrical moral based on the dignity of the human being and the freedom of conscience. A splendid masterpiece of obscurity and ambiguity.

August 21: Father Coache, probably the last great figure of the old resistance in France, dies peacefully. A doctor in Canon Law and parish priest for many years, his bishop expelled him for continuing the traditional procession of Corpus Christi in his parish. With his publications, his pilgrimages to Rome and to Lourdes, Father Coache was a great supporter of the traditional cause.

1995

The Old Guard goes and leaves the work to the young soldiers. On May 12, Father Barcelonne dies in France at ninety-four years of age. He worked for twenty-seven years in China from where he was expelled in 1952 by the Communists. Missionary in Brazil; guess the diocese. Campos, all right. He returned to France and spent his last ten years at St. Nicolas du Chardonnet, where he was affectionately called "The Patriarch." He finishes his testament by writing: "The only grace I ask is to die in an act of perfect love and total abandonment in the infinite mercy of God." He was faithful until the end to the Mass of his seventy-three years of priesthood.

Fr. Urban Snyder, from the Abbey of Gethsemani, where he had been master of novices, dies January 25. He was one of the priests who were incardinated in the Society of Saint Pius X by rescript of the Sacred Congregation of Religious. From 1972 to 1976 he taught at Ecône.

The Papal Encyclical *Ut Unum Sint* consecrates the ecumenical mania under the inadmissible belief that "The spirit of Christ uses non-Catholic churches as means of salvation." After Vatican II, ecumenism was a pious wish; after *Ut Unum Sint* ecumenism is a command for the whole Church.

Fr. Urban Snyder (right), "The Kentucky Pilgrim," visited the American seminaries in Ridgefield and Winona several times in his last years. (See *The Angelus*, April 1995.)

1996

The second theological congress of *SìSìNoNo* was held at the Society's house in Albano, Italy on "The problems posed for the Catholic conscience by the last Council." Fifty-five seminarians and priests, including three bishops attended.

Bishop Fabian Bruskewitz of Lincoln, Nebraska, decides to make use of an "old-fashioned" ecclesiastical penalty and excommunicates several non- and anti-Catholic groups in his diocese. While some saw his denunciation of groups such as the Freemasons and Planned Parenthood as a breath of fresh air, His Excellency included the Society of St. Pius X's mission in Lincoln in his list of forbidden organizations. Such a situation provides a sad commentary on the state of the "new springtime" of the conciliar Church.

Roughly five years after the death of Archbishop Lefebvre, Bishop Bernard Tissier de Mallerais is charged with penning a biography of the founder of the Society of St. Pius X.

On October 22, 1996, Pope John Paul II addressed the Pontifical Academy of Sciences:

My predecessor Pius XII has already affirmed that there is no conflict between evolution and the doctrine of the faith regarding man and his vocation, provided that we do not lose sight of certain fixed points....Today, more than a half-century after the appearance of that encyclical, some new findings lead us toward the recognition of evolution as more than an hypothesis. In fact it is remarkable that this theory has had progressively greater influence on the spirit of researchers, following a series of discoveries in different scholarly disciplines. The convergence in the results of these independent studies–which was neither planned nor sought–constitutes in itself a significant argument in favor of the theory.

Bishop Tissier de Mallerais' authoritative biography of Archbishop Lefebvre. Over seven hundred pages long, it contains the details of his long and fruitful life, from his family in France, through his years as a missionary and, of course, his work as founder of the Society.

At the annual priestly ordinations in Ecône, Switzerland, Bishop Salvador Lazo (fourth from right) formally participates in the ceremony. He was a retired diocesan bishop from the Philippines.

Nine priests are ordained for the Society of St. Pius X at St. Thomas Aquinas Seminary in Winona, Minnesota.

Bishop Salvador Lazo from the Philippines attends the priestly ordinations at St. Pius X Seminary in Ecône.

1997

In May of 1997, the Bishop of Sion in Switzerland presented two texts that purportedly were official documents from Rome which declared that the SSPX and its adherents were in "formal schism" due to the 1988 Consecrations. However, neither of the texts were signed, dated or listed with the required Vatican Protocol Number. The SSPX then made an investigation into the matter; at the end of the year the Vatican published the texts!

1998

In October, Msgr. Perl issues a letter which states:

> While it is true that participation in the Mass at the chapels of the Society of St. Pius X does not of itself constitute "formal adherence to the schism", such adherence can come about over a period of time as one slowly imbibes a schismatic mentality which separates itself

from the teaching of the Supreme Pontiff and the entire Catholic Church.

On October 10, the new church at the seminary of Ecône is blessed. Almost 100 priests and 3,000 faithful attend the magnificent ceremonies.

The magnificent new seminary church in Ecône

1999

In January, the municipality of Turin, Italy, authorizes Muslims to hold a public prayer service for Ramadan. A conservative Italian political party calls the SSPX to offer a public Mass in reparation. Father Simoulin does so, in the presence of nearly 800 people, many of which were introduced to Tradition by this event.

Division arises in the Fraternity of St. Peter as 16 priests wrote a letter to Rome attacking the other members for being too rigidly attached to the rites of 1962. At the same time, the Congregation for Divine Worship declared, on July 3, that every Ecclesia Dei priest can, and in certain circumstances, must celebrate the New Mass, as well as concelebrating it, and that none of their superiors can oppose this.

The Society continues to spread in Eastern Europe, as Bishop Fellay joins Belorussia, Russia and Ukraine to the District of Austria. Bishop Tissier de Mallerais confers confirmations in the Czech Republic, the first time the Society has performed such a ceremony there. A house in Albania is attempted, although various acts of violence will eventually force the Society to abandon this mission. The first Czech priest is ordained by Bishop de Galarreta.

In France, Father Laurençon institutes a Letter to Fellow Priests. This regular initiative is sent to every priest in France. He receives over 300 responses to the introductory letter.

Bishop Williamson founds the year of Humanities at the seminary in Winona. Incoming seminarians would henceforth take an entrance examination; those who did not pass would take a year of the liberal arts, including the study of music, literature, Latin, and history.

News in Asia: The District Houses moves from Manila in the Philippines to Singapore in order to be more centrally locat-

(Top left) **Bishop Bernard Fellay in the Philippines.**
(Top right) **St. Bernard's Pre-seminary and Novitiate in Ilo Ilo, Philippines.**
(Left) **The Oblates of the Society continue to grow, prompting their novitiate to be moved from Menzingen to an old school in Salvan, Switzerland.**

(Left) Bishop Fellay and Bishop Lazo.
(Right) The three children of Fatima.

ed. St. Bernard's, a pre-seminary and novitiate, is founded in the Philippines. At the initiative of Father Onoda, Archbishop Lefebvre is published in Korean for the first time.

The Oblates of the Society continue to grow, prompting their novitiate to be moved from Menzingen to an old school in Salvan, Switzerland.

On October 31, the "Common Declaration on Justification" is published by the Catholic Church and the Lutherans simultaneously. This document is a masterpiece in ambiguity, further confusing an already complicated issue.

A second Day of Prayer is held in Assisi, similar to the first one in 1986. Like the first occasion, this ecumenical endeavor was a reminder to traditional Catholics that little had changed when it came to doctrinal innovations.

2000

On January 18, Pope John Paul opens the Holy Door at St. Paul Outside the Walls for the Jubilee. Even this becomes an ecumenical opportunity as "six hands" jointly open the doors, including representatives from the Orthodox and the Anglicans.

In February, Fathers Couture and Wailliez go to Vietnam for the first time. Although the political climate makes such visits dangerous, there is much reason for hope in the apostolate there.

On March 12, Pope John Paul II apologies, on behalf of Catholics everywhere, for various "sins" the Church has committed throughout history. The offenses include the Inquisition and the Crusades.

Bishop Lazo passes to his eternal reward in April. However, Bishop John Bosco Chuabsamai Manat, bishop of the Diocese of Ratchaburi, Thailand, begins to collaborate with the SSPX, even offering Mass at the seminary in Ecône.

Cardinal Hoyos becomes President of the Ecclesia Dei committee. The Society remembers that it was he who once bragged to Archbishop Lefebvre that he had helped implement religious liberty into the concordat with Colombia, his native land! He is, however, known to have some sympathy to the old Mass liturgically.

In August, the Society leads a Pilgrimage of Tradition to Rome for the Jubilee Year. Over 5,000 faithful attend in addition to the bishops of the Society and hundreds of priests. This pilgrimage seems to leave a favorable impression in the minds of many in Rome.

In 2000, for the Holy Year Jubilee, the SSPX made a "Pilgrimage of Tradition" to Rome. The hundreds of priests (many of which seen here, in St. Peter's Square), and the thousands of faithful, left a favorable impression on the Roman authorities.

The Third Secret of Fatima is released, amidst much speculation and controversy. Many point out problems with this official release, indicating that part may still be missing. The release and interpretation of the Third Secret seems to stoke the fires it intended to quell.

The Society continues to expand in America, opening a priory in Syracuse, New York.

Bishop Tissier de Mallerais takes up residence at the seminary in Ecône.

On August 6, the document *Dominus Iesus* is issued, on the unicity and salvific universality of Our Lord and the Church. Signed by Cardinal Ratzinger, it limits some of the excesses of Pope John Paul II while pleasing neither side. Ultimately, it resolves nothing.

The Society of St. Pius X reaches two more milestones. During this year, for the first time, the number of priests tops 400. The entire Society celebrates their 30th anniversary as a religious community.

On September 3, Pius IX and Dom Columba Marmion are beatified by Pope John Paul II. Unfortunately, in the same ceremony, John XXIII receives the same honor, even though due process was not observed.

In an effort to combat the rampant ecumenism and other doctrinal problems present as well in the Eastern Catholic Church, the Society of St. Josaphat is founded in the Ukraine to work alongside the SSPX. Their first superior is Fr. Vasyl Kovpack and they found a seminary.

The Society of St. Josaphat, an Eastern-rite group of traditionalists in the Ukraine, works for Tradition alongside the SSPX.

2001

In February, the Society presents a study on the New Mass to Pope John Paul II. It is entitled *The Problem of the Liturgical Reform*. In the Foreword, Bishop

(Left) Seminary church, La Reja, Argentina.
(Above) St. Joseph's, Brussels, Belgium.

Fellay writes: "We strongly be-
seech Your Holiness, who alone
has the power as Successor of
Peter and Shepherd of the universal Church, to strengthen
his brethren in the faith and to
sanction with his apostolic authority the indispensable clari-
fications which are demanded
by the present tragic situation
in the Church."

St. Isidore's, Denver, Colorado

DICI (International Catholic Documentation and Information)
is founded as the official communication agency of the Society.
Through DICI, the SSPX provides regular information as well as
analysis of the events and documents pertaining to the life of the
Church.

The Pontifical Council for Promoting Christian Unity (PCPCU)
issues a document on the mutual admission to the Eucharist of the
Chaldean Catholic Church and the Assyrian (Nestorian) Church.
There is a problem, however: The Assyrians celebrate a liturgy known
as the Liturgy of Addai and Mari, in which there are no words of
consecration. With this document, the PCPCU claims that such a

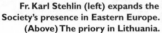
Fr. Karl Stehlin (left) expands the Society's presence in Eastern Europe. (Above) The priory in Lithuania.

liturgy is valid nonetheless, a true revolution in sacramental theology.: Bishop Fellay says that the justification given by Cardinal Ratzinger, namely that words of consecration are found here and there in the Assyrian rite *"Anaphora,"* undermines the Catholic doctrine of the sacraments.

In the winter, convinced that the overtures from Rome since the Pilgrimage of Tradition are worthy of consideration and reflection, the priests of Campos decide to strike a deal, going against the Society's course of action. At first, they claim they want to remain friends, but as the Society argues, they will slowly abandon the fight for Tradition. History has already demonstrated who was right.

In America, St. Isidore's in Denver, Colorado, is finished and blessed. It is arguably the most beautiful of the Society's churches in the United States. Not to be outdone in Europe, however, the Society acquires St. Joseph's in Brussels, Belgium, an edifice bigger even than St. Nicholas in Paris! In Argentina, the Society blesses the church at the seminary in La Reja.

2002

In April, Msgr. Camille Perl, Secretary of the Pontifical Commission Ecclesia Dei, published a response to the question whether one can assist at the Masses offered by priests of the SSPX. He replied in the negative, alleging that they are in schism.

In June, Padre Pio is canonized.

Also in June, a schismatic bishop (Romulo Antonio Braschi) in Passau "ordained" seven women. The Holy See issued a monitum (Congregation for the Doctrine of the Faith, July 10, 2002) informing the women that the ordination was null and void, and urging them to repent. They resisted.

In July, *L'Osservatore Romano* confirms the election of Father Rifan as bishop of the Apostolic Administration of the St. John Marie Vianney Society. He is to be consecrated bishop in the Cathedral of Campos on August 18, 2002. The ordination is to be conferred by Dario Cardinal Castrillon Hoyos assisted by Bishop Guimaraes, the local Ordinary.

St. Mary's Academy and College, under Father Anglés, launches an apostolate new to the Society: a radio station! At 98.3 FM, for roughly twenty-five miles around St. Marys Kansas, one can hear traditional Catholic sermons, devotions, and conferences.

Fr. Karl Stehlin, of the Society's apostolate in Eastern Europe, restores St. Maximilian Kolbe's Militia Immaculatæ. A priory is also opened in Lithuania, further solidifying the work of the Society there.

A view of the 25th-anniversary celebrations at St. Marys, Kansas

Bishop Rifan is consecrated for the priests of Campos after the death of Bishop Rangel. They are thus the first community under the Ecclesia Dei umbrella to be granted a bishop.

2003

In April, Pope John Paul II's encyclical *Ecclesia de Eucharistia* is published.

The Society opens its newest African apostolate in Kenya.

In March, the British District of the SSPX founds *Mater Dei*, a new journal dedicated to the spread of Tradition in England.

In Argentina, in response to a potential liberalization of the laws against abortion, some priests of the Society found the "Foundation of the 25th of March" in honor of the Incarnation of the Word of God in the womb of the Blessed Virgin. This group is a catalyst for the maintenance of the anti-abortion laws in Argentina.

In April, St. Bernard's Novitiate in the Philippines is vandalized and robbed; Brother Hyacinthe is shot in the process but recovers. It is a reminder of the real danger these missionaries face!

Campos: True to the Society's prediction, the priests of Campos start to waver in their adherence to Tradition. Bishop Rifan assists in Niteroi-Rio at the *Novus Ordo* Requiem Mass of the Cardinal of Rio and receives Communion.

Two Romes: In October, a three day ecumenical conference is held in Fatima. On the other hard, Cardinal Hoyos offers Mass in the Tridentine rite, angering liberals and encouraging traditionalists.

Cardinal Hoyos, then President of the Ecclesia Dei Commission, offers a public Tridentine Mass.

Pope John Paul II introduces the "Luminous Mysteries" of the Rosary. It is not so much the introduction of a new rosary which is so revolutionary (as there are a variety of rosaries in the Church) but that these supplant some of the traditional mysteries, or at least the days on which they are prayed.

Missionary work is not confined to Eastern Europe; in Asia, There are some contacts with China.

The Society celebrates the centenary of St. Pius X's election to the Pontificate with a variety of conferences, celebrations, and studies. Providentially, the Society crosses another milestone; they now number more than 450 priests.

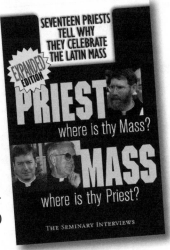

The U.S. District sends a copy of this book to every priest in the United States.

St. Mary's Academy and College celebrates its 25th anniversary. The Governor of the State of Kansas, by official proclamation, declares it "St. Mary's Academy and College" Day. The school year begins with 775 students enrolled, easily the biggest school in the Society.

Father Roch passes away, leaving behind a legacy of fruitful work in the vineyard of the Lord.

2004

In May, Hindus were allowed to perform a "prayer for peace" at the Catholic altar at the Shrine in Fatima.

The SSPX interviews seventeen priests—none of whom are members of the SSPX—about why they remained faithful to the traditional Mass, learned how to say it, or came to Tradition. They send these interviews in book form to all 46,000 priests in America. Many hundreds of priests respond asking for further information.

Following on their liturgical study, on the occasion of the 25th anniversary of the pontificate of Pope John Paul II, Bishop Fellay addressed the cardinals of the Roman Catholic Church in a letter about the disastrous effects of ecumenism effected through Vatican

(Top left) Notre Dame de La Salette Boys Academy is opened in Olivet, Illinois. (Top right) The General Chapter re-elects Bishop Bernard Fellay as Superior General. Fr. Niklaus Pfluger is elected First Assistant and Fr. Marc-Alain Nély, Second Assistant. (Right) The SSPX makes a pilgrimage of reparation to Fatima in 2005.

II and the *Novus Ordo Missae.* Included with the letter was the study *From Ecumenism to Silent Apostasy.*

In December, Pope John Paul II declared the beatification of Charles de Foucauld could proceed.

2005

On April 2, after nearly twenty-seven years as the Vicar of Christ, Pope John Paul II passed away.

On April 19, Cardinal Joseph Ratzinger was elected to the papacy. He takes the name of Benedict XVI.

On May 13, Benedict XVI announced the opening of the cause of beatification of John Paul II. The rescript is dated May 9.

The Society opens its second priory in Ireland. Located in Athlone, in the center of the country, it is hoped that a second priory will help spread the work of the Society in the Land of Saints and Scholars.

Notre Dame de La Salette Boys Academy is opened in America. A boarding boys' high school, it is the first of its kind. Following a strict liberal arts curriculum, and with the ability for young men to be around priests and the Sacrifice daily, many vocations should come from it.

The SSPX in Britain mails a video, brochure and letter about the old Mass and Tradition to all 5,000 priests in the country.

In August, the Society leads a pilgrimage of reparation to Fatima.

In an interview, Cardinal Hoyos, President of the Ecclesia Dei commission, publicly states that the situation of the Society is "not one of formal schism."

On December 22, Pope Benedict gives his famous address to the Curia, encouraging them to follow a "hermeneutics of continuity" and not a "hermeneutics of rupture" when interpreting the documents of Vatican II. This sparks much discussion on all sides of the Catholic spectrum.

2006

Pope Benedict XVI, formerly Joseph Cardinal Ratzinger

On January 25, Pope Benedict XVI issues his first encyclical, *Deus Caritas Est.*

The Third General Chapter of the Society of St. Pius X meets in Ecône and re-elects Bishop Bernard Fellay as Superior General. Father Niklaus Pfluger is elected First Assistant and Father Marc-Alain Nély, Second Assistant.

In October, a letter by the Congregation for Divine Worship (Cardinal Arinze,

The SSPX leads a pilgrimage to Lourdes. During the homily of the main Mass, Bishop Fellay announces a second Rosary Crusade for the lifting of the excommunications.

Prefect) was sent to the bishops' conferences, ordering that the words "*pro multis*" henceforth be translated as "for many" instead of "for all."

Yet another group of former SSPX priests forms a new Ecclesia Dei organization: The Institute of the Good Shepherd.

2007

On July 7, the Apostolic Letter *Summorum Pontificum* was published, freeing the Mass, meeting the first preliminary of the SSPX for the opening of doctrinal discussions. A *Te Deum* was sung in the churches of the SSPX for thanksgiving.

2008

In October, the SSPX leads a pilgrimage to Lourdes. Some estimate the crowd at over 20,000 souls. During the homily of the main

Mass, Bishop Fellay announces a second Rosary Crusade for the lifting of the excommunications of 1988.

2009

On January 21, Pope Benedict XVI remits the "excommunications" of the four bishops. This fulfills the second condition the Society had requested. The way is now paved for doctrinal discussions.

2010

While modern Rome descends deeper and deeper into the darkness of confusion, the Society of Saint Pius X calmly, quietly and securely perseveres in the luminous work of preaching Our Lord crucified and guiding souls to heaven.

Archbishop Lefebvre outside
the cathedral in Dakar

In the preface of his *Spiritual Journey*, the Archbishop wrote a mysterious and unusual paragraph:

Before entering into the bosom of the Holy Trinity, I will be allowed to realize the dream of which God gave me a glimpse one day in the cathedral of Dakar. The dream was to transmit, before the progressive degradation of the priestly ideal, in all of its doctrinal purity and in all of its missionary charity, the Catholic priesthood of our Lord Jesus Christ, just as He conferred it on His Apostles, just as the Roman Church always transmitted it until the middle of the twentieth century.

The dream is now a reality. By its fortieth anniversary, the Society of Saint Pius X numbers 4 bishops, 529 priests, 233 seminarians, 104 brothers, about 160 sisters, and 73 oblates, living in 183 houses in 32 countries. Together they seek the goal of the priesthood: the glorification of God, the continuation of Our Lord's redemptive work, the salvation of souls. They accomplish this by fidelity to Christ's testament—the Holy Sacrifice of the Mass.

A facsimile of the holy card of Archbishop Lefebvre's ordination to the priesthood reprinted on the occasion of the 25th anniversary of the Society of Saint Pius X. It says:

Do this in memory of Me.

Receive the power to offer to God the Holy Sacrifice, and to celebrate the Holy Mass for the living and the dead in the name of the Lord. Amen.

The Society's Presence in the United States (2010)

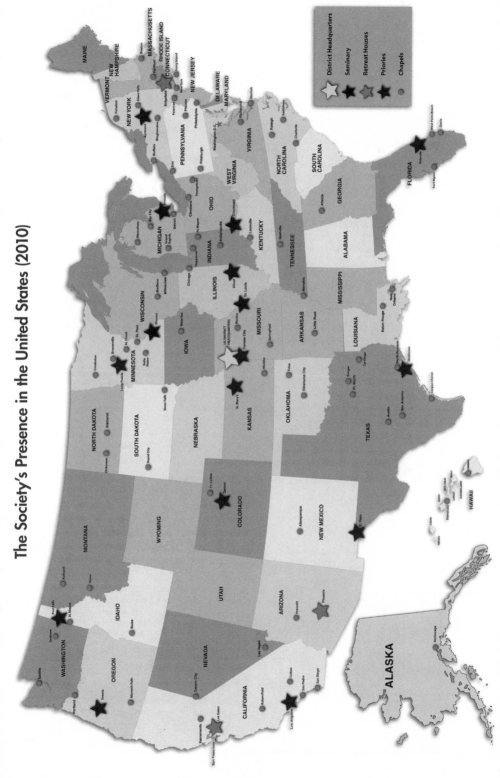